Everyman's Poetry

Everyman, I will go with thee,
and be thy guide

Oscar Wilde

Selected and edited by ROBERT MIGHALL

University of Oxford

EVERYMAN
J. M. Dent · London

Selection, introduction and other critical apparatus
© J. M. Dent 1996

J. M. Dent
Orion Publishing Group
Orion House
5 Upper St Martin's Lane
London WC2H 9EA

Typeset by Deltatype Ltd, Ellesmere Port, Cheshire
Printed in Great Britain by
The Guernsey Press Co. Ltd, Guernsey, C.I.

British Library Cataloguing-in-Publication
Data is available upon request.

ISBN 0 460 87803 4

Contents

Note on the Author and Editor

OSCAR WILDE was born in Dublin on 16 October 1854, the son of a surgeon and a poet. He was educated at Trinity College, Dublin, and Magdalen College, Oxford, where he won the Newdigate Prize with a poem called 'Ravenna', and also became the leader of the so-called aesthetic cult. His first volume of poems was published in 1881. In 1884 he married Constance Lloyd, and in 1888 he published *The Happy Prince*, a volume of fairy tales written for his sons. His only novel, *The Picture of Dorian Gray*, aroused outrage when it appeared in 1890 and was denounced by some critics as 'immoral'. His first theatrical success was *Lady Windermere's Fan* in 1892; this was followed by *A Woman of No Importance* (1893). *An Ideal Husband* and *The Importance of Being Earnest* both appeared in 1895. But that same year also saw his downfall when he lost a libel action against the Marquess of Queensbury, whose son Lord Alfred Douglas he had been infatuated with since 1891. Wilde was subsequently charged and sentenced to two years' imprisonment for homosexual offences, which led to his social and financial ruin. After his release he went to live in France where he wrote *The Ballad of Reading Gaol* (1898), which was inspired by his experience in prison. He died in Paris on 30 November 1900.

ROBERT MIGHALL is a Junior Research Fellow in English at Merton College, Oxford. He has published in various journals on aspects of nineteenth-century culture, including pieces on Oscar Wilde. His doctorate was on Victorian Gothic fiction and Criminology. He is currently revising this for publication.

Chronology of Wilde's Life

Year	Age	Life
1854		Born in Dublin 16 October
1864–71	10–17	Attends Portora Royal School, Enniskillen

Chronology of his Times

Year	Artistic Events	Historical Events
1854–6		Crimean War
1856	Flaubert, *Madame Bovary*	
1857	Baudelaire, *Les fleurs du mal*	Indian rising ('Mutiny')
	Elizabeth Barrett Browning, *Aurora Leigh*	
1859	Darwin, *The Origin of Species*	
	Tennyson, *Idylls of the King*	
1861–5		American Civil War
1862	Whistler's 'Symphony in White, No. 1: The White Girl' exhibited	
1864	Browning, *Dramatis Personae*	
	Newman, *Apologia pro Vita Sua*	
1865	Arnold, *Essays in Criticism*	President Lincoln assassinated
1866	Swinburne, *Poems and Ballads*	Nobel invents dynamite
1868	Browning, *The Ring and the Book*	Gladstone becomes Prime Minister
1869	Arnold, *Culture and Anarchy*	College for Women opens in Cambridge
		Von Kertbeny coins the term 'Homosexuality'
1870	D. G. Rossetti, *Poems*	Franco–Prussian War (to 1871)
	Death of Dickens	Elementary Education Act

Year	Age	Life
1871–4	17–20	Reading Classics at Trinity College, Dublin. Granted scholarship to Magdalen College, Oxford
1874–8	20–24	At Oxford, starts contributing poems to literary journals. Takes First in Classical Moderations (1876) and in Literae Humaniores (1878). Wins the Newdigate Prize for Poetry with 'Ravenna', which he publishes the same year
1879	25	Moves to London, as self-styled 'professor of aesthetics'
1881	27	*Poems* published
1882	28	Lectures in North America. Revised *Poems* published
1883	29	Spends three months in Paris. His first play, *Vera; Or the Nihilist*, produced in New York
1884	30	Marries Constance Lloyd; moves to Chelsea. Begins regular book-reviewing

Year	Artistic Events	Historical Events
1871	Eliot, *Middlemarch*	Trade Unions legalised
	Swinburne, *Songs before Sunrise*	Paris Commune
1872	Robert Buchanan, *The Fleshly School of Poetry*	
1873	Pater, *Studies in the History of the Renaissance*	
1874	Flaubert, *Temptation of St Antony*	Disraeli becomes Prime Minister
	Monet's 'Impression: Sunrise' exhibited	
	Eliot, *Daniel Deronda*	
1877	Grosvenor Gallery opened	Queen Victoria made Empress of India
	W. H. Mallock, *The New Republic*	
1878	Hardy, *The Return of the Native*	London electric street lighting established
1879	Meredith, *The Egoist*	London telephone exchange established
	Ibsen, *A Doll's House*	
1880	Death of George Eliot	Gladstone becomes (Liberal) Prime Minister
1881	James, *The Portrait of a Lady*	Irish Land Law Act
	Ibsen, *Ghosts*	
	D. G. Rossetti, *Ballads and Sonnets*	
	Gilbert and Sullivan's *Patience* is produced	
1882	Walter Hamilton, *The Aesthetic Movement in England*	Irish Chief Secretary assassinated
		Married Women's Property Act
1883	R. L. Stevenson, *Treasure Island*	Karl Marx dies
1884	J-K Huysmans, *A Rebours*	The Mahdi takes Omdurman

Year	Age	Life
1885	31	Son Cyril born
1886	32	Son Vyvyan born. Wilde meets Robert Ross
1887–9	33–35	Editor of *Woman's World* monthly magazine
1888	34	*The Happy Prince and Other Tales* published
1890	36	First version of *The Picture of Dorian Gray* published
1891	37	*The Duchess of Padua* – with the title *Guido Ferranti* – produced in New York. Meets Lord Alfred Douglas. Publishes the revised *Dorian Gray, Intentions, Lord Arthur Savile's Crime and Other Stories* and *A House of Pomegranates*. Visits Paris (meets Gide, Proust and Mallarmé)
1892	38	*Lady Windermere's Fan* produced. London production of *Salomé* refused theatre licence.
1893	39	*Salomé* published in English translation. *The Sphinx* and *A Woman of No Importance* published

Year	Artistic Events	Historical Events
1885	Pater, *Marius the Epicurean*	Berlin Conference
		Gordon dies at Khartoum
	Whistler delivers his 'Ten O'Clock Lecture'	Criminal Law Amendment Act (against homosexual practices)
1886	R. L. Stevenson, *Dr Jekyll and Mr Hyde*	Gladstone re-elected
		Irish Home Rule Bill defeated
	Krafft-Ebbing, *Psychopathia Sexualis*	
1887	Pater, *Imaginary Portraits*	Queen Victoria's Golden Jubilee
1888	Arnold, *Essays in Criticism* (second series)	Local Government Act
		Eastman's Kodak box camera
	Death of Arnold	
1889	Pater, *Appreciations*	Cleveland Street scandal over homosexual brothels
	Yeats, *The Wanderings of Oisin*	Parnell named in O'Shea divorce case
1890	Ibsen, *Hedda Gabler*	Parnell resigns as Irish Nationalist leader
	James, *The Tragic Muse*	
	Death of Newman	
1891	Hardy, *Tess of the D'Urbevilles*	
	Morris, *News from Nowhere*	
1892	Kipling, *Barrack Room Ballads*	Gladstone's fourth Ministry
	Death of Whitman	
	Death of Tennyson	
1893	Pater, *Plato and Platonism*	Independent Labour Party formed
		Lords reject Irish Home Rule Bill

Year	Age	Life
1895	41	*An Ideal Husband* and *The Importance of Being Earnest* produced. Wilde unsuccessfully sues the Marquess of Queensbury for criminal libel. Wilde charged with 'acts of gross indecency with other male persons'. A first trial fails to deliver a unanimous verdict. Wilde is found guilty at the second trial and given two years hard labour, served at Holloway, Pentonville, Wandsworth and Reading Gaol
1896	42	Death of mother. *Salomé* produced in Paris
1897	43	Writes *De Profundis* in prison. On release settles at Bernevale, near Dieppe, then visits Italy with Douglas
1898	44	*The Ballad of Reading Gaol* published. Moves to Paris. Death of Constance Wilde
1899	45	*The Importance of Being Earnest* and *An Ideal Husband* published. Travels in Europe
1900	46	Visits Rome and Naples. Returns to Paris. Baptized a Roman Catholic during severe illness. Dies 30 November

Year	Artistic Events	Historical Events
1894	Pater, *The Child in the House* Shaw, *Arms and the Man* First issue of *The Yellow Book* (to 1897)	Trial of Dreyfus in Paris Gladstone resigns
1895	Hardy, *Jude the Obscure* Pater, *Greek Studies* Yeats, *Poems* Max Nordau's *Degeneration* (1893) translated into English	Lumière Brothers invent cinematography Jameson Raid into the Transvaal
1896	A. E. Houseman, *A Shropshire Lad*	
1897	James, *What Maisie Knew* Havelock Ellis, *Sexual Inversion*	Queen Victoria's Diamond Jubilee Second Colonial Conference
1898	Hardy, *Wessex Poems* James, *The Turn of the Screw* Shaw, *Mrs Warren's Profession*	Kitchener defeats Dervishes at Omdurman
1899	A. Symons, *The Symbolist Movement in Literature* Yeats, *The Wind Among the Reeds*	Outbreak of the Boer War
1900	Conrad, *Lord Jim* Shaw, *Three Plays for Puritans* Death of Ruskin	British Labour Party founded Relief of Ladysmith and Mafeking

Introduction

The biographical 'facts' about Oscar Wilde the poet can be dealt with in relatively few sentences. He started contributing poems to periodicals while still at Oxford, and in 1878 he won the Newdigate Poetry Prize with 'Ravenna'. In 1881 he published *Poems* at his own expense. This he revised slightly and re-issued the following year. During the 1880s, while he was making his name as a lecturer, journalist, essayist and fiction writer, he published a handful of poems in various journals. *The Sphinx* appeared in 1894. And, following his two years' imprisonment, Wilde published his final poem, *The Ballad of Reading Gaol* in 1898.

Wilde's reputation as a poet is almost as slight as its biographical outline. When the Oxford Union rejected the 1881 *Poems*, having themselves originally solicited it, they set the tone for subsequent critical opinion. The major charge was that of plagiarism; and echoes of this response have sounded well into the present century, with criticism often resembling a game of 'snap', as the critic matches the poet's 'borrowing' with his or her own comprehensive knowledge of Wilde's sources. The notion of Wilde the poet, when compared with Wilde the playwright, paradoxist or personality, is rarely given serious consideration. And yet Wilde considered poets to be the 'supreme' artists, and to the end counted himself among them. Shortly before his death he prophesied that he would be remembered as 'the Infamous St Oscar of Oxford, Poet and Martyr' (*Letters*, p. 720). We have readily accepted the latter distinction, so why not the former? Perhaps the notion that this aspect of Wilde's life and work can be excused, ignored or discounted needs to be re-examined. Wilde the poet ought to be given a hearing.

In 1868 the critic Walter Pater published a review of William Morris's poetry (this he revised, and published as 'Aesthetic Poetry' in 1889). This is how Pater characterises such poetry: 'Of that world [already transfigured by poetry] this new poetry takes possession, and sublimates beyond it another still fainter and more spectral, which is literally an artificial or "earthly paradise". It is a finer ideal, extracted from what in relation to any actual world is

already an ideal. Like some strange second flowering after date, it
renews on a more delicate type the poetry of a past age, but must
not be confounded with it' (Pater, p.300). This description could be
applied to many of the poems found in Wilde's first volume,
produced when the author was most under the influence of Pater.
Like Morris's 'extraction' from Medieval romance, Wilde's
'ballades', 'villanelles' and elaborate Ovidian narratives 'renew on'
poetry of the past, mastering earlier forms and adapting them to
new uses. Thus 'The Garden of Eros' (1881) adopts a genre which
owes much to the examples of Chaucer and Spenser, infuses this
with Keatsian imagery and Arnoldian pastoral topography, and
cultivates what is largely a defence of the Aesthetic ideal in the face
of mercantile, industrial and scientific 'philistinism'. Wilde would
champion this cause throughout his career, and 'The Garden of
Eros' provides an early and self-consciously artistic, or even
'artificial', articulation of it. Significantly, Morris is among those
whom the poem eulogises for carrying the torch of the 'Spirit of
Beauty'. To such writers the young poet explicitly acknowledges a
debt. This debt was perhaps a version of the aestheticised appropri-
ation which Pater attributes to Morris. Wilde's lines on Morris from
this poem can perhaps be considered in this light. Here Morris is
hymned as the 'heritor of Spenser's tuneful reed', and the
progenitor of further verse:

> . . . how oft, in some cool grassy field
>
> Far from the cricket-ground and noisy eight,
>   At Bagley, where the rustling bluebells come
> Almost before the blackbird finds a mate
> . . . Have I lain poring on the dreamy tales his fancy weaves,
>
> And through their unreal woes and mimic pain
>   Wept for myself, and so was purified,
> And in their simple mirth grew glad again;
>   For as I sailed upon that pictured tide
> The strength and splendour of the storm was mine
> Without the storm's red ruin, for the singer is divine,
>
> ('Eros', 174–86)

Here we find perhaps a semi-autobiographical vignette of the
fledgling poet at Oxford, absorbing the influence of a master, but

also developing the aesthetic which both defends his present poetic practice, and which would later form the basis of his critical theory. As Vivian in 'The Decay of Lying' declares: 'To us, who live in the nineteenth century, any century is a suitable subject for art except our own. The only beautiful things are the things that do not concern us. It is . . . exactly because Hecuba is nothing to us that her sorrows are so suitable a motive for a tragedy' (*Intentions*, pp. 53–4). Thus the 'strength and splendour' of another poet's art becomes his own, and the 'unreal woes' which are, in Pater's words 'already an ideal', provide strange second flowerings in Wilde's 'Garden of Eros'. To call this approach plagiarism, and to lay the charge of insincerity which such an accusation implies, is perhaps to disregard the spirit in which such verse was written, and to misunderstand the principles of the 'Aestheticism' which Wilde was self-consciously advocating at this time.

The modern critic's concurrence with those who rejected Wilde's first poetic offerings also overlooks the fact that Wilde developed as a poet, and that this development mirrors that of his artistic culture in general. Even within the first volume of 1881 there is evidence that the author was experimenting with new forms, and that he was refining his poetic according to his own understanding of its strengths and weaknesses. *Poems* is divided into a number of sections which accommodate its various modes and genres. Thus the 'devotional' poems of the 'Rosa Mystica' section, produced while he was attracted to Roman Catholicism, offer a contrast to the more abstract 'Impressions', most of which were written in 1881 and placed in the 'Wind Flowers', 'Flowers of Gold' and 'The Fourth Movement' sections of *Poems*. Wilde's development as a poet is also evident in his revision of poems that had appeared earlier. 'By the Arno' is a case in point. It was originally part of a longer poem entitled 'Graffiti D'Italia. San Miniato. (June 15)' from 1876, the first part of which would later appear as 'San Miniato'. Wilde's division of the original poem, and his placing each part in different sections of the 1881 volume, was appropriate, and testifies to his understanding of his own development. 'San Miniato' retains the 'occasional' and devotional qualities of the earlier poem. It still describes a significant event, a form of pilgrimage. The beauties of the church and its surroundings are subordinate to the prayer to the Virgin which the occasion brings forth. 'By the Arno', on the other hand, is largely descriptive. The interest is in the beauty of the Florentine setting, and in capturing its atmosphere. And whilst the poem is not yet purely descriptive (as Wilde's later 'Impressionistic' poems would strive to be), its more Romantic elements, such as the inclusion of the nightingale as motif for the poet's 'heart's delight', are unobtrusive and evocative of mood, rather than strictly symbolic or allegorical. Hence he places 'By the Arno' in the 'Flowers of Gold' section, alongside more self-consciously 'Aesthetic' pieces such as 'Les Silhouettes' and 'In the Gold Room'.

Wilde continued to experiment in the mode represented by these latter poems. In the 'Impressionistic' and 'Symbolist' pieces he produced between 1882 and his imprisonment in 1895, he found his poetic niche. In poems such as 'Le Jardin', 'Le Panneau' and 'Symphony in Yellow', Wilde purged his art of the rhapsodic extravagance and overwrought imagery which mars some of his earlier poems. Where once he sought abundance, he now seeks precision, restraint and an economical evocation of mood, atmosphere and effect. Where his verse was once florid, it is now bejewelled and consciously artificial. Wilde's verse was always 'pictorial'; like Keats he appealed to the eye as well as to the ear. In his later poems, however, his idiom is often explicitly 'painterly', inviting analogies with the work produced at this time by the French Impressionists and their English counterparts Whistler and Walter Sickert. 'Symphony in Yellow' (1889) is a cityscape, suffused with the soft lights and shades of the Impressionistic palate:

> Big barges full of yellow hay
> > Are moored against the shadowy wharf,
> > And, like a yellow silken scarf,
> The thick fog hangs along the quay.

If, as Vivian in 'The Decay of Lying' suggests, the Impressionists were responsible for the London fogs – 'To whom, if not to them and their master, do we owe the lovely silver mists that brood over our river, and turn to faint forms of fading grace curved bridge and swaying barge?' (*Intentions*, p. 40) – then Wilde's poem observes their effects through these painters' eyes, producing an artistically mediated rendering of atmospheric effect.

Wilde was not solely preoccupied with the abstract ideals of literary Impressionism during this period. The late 1880s and 90s also witnessed his experiments in modes with which he has come to be firmly associated – Symbolism and Decadence. 'The Harlot's House' (1885) – with its attention to sound as well as image, and it's grotesque allegories of lust and shame – best illustrates Wilde's 'Symbolist' phase; while *The Sphinx* (1894) remains perhaps one of the few poems in English which can rightly claim the epithet *Décadent*. Here, the esoteria, erudition and ornate eroticism of the French masters of this mode (Baudelaire in poetry, Huysmans in prose and Gustave Moreau in painting) find their most consummate British practitioner. It is a mode which suited Wilde's particular talents. *The Sphinx* is an extended erotic reverie, but also a catalogue of the bizarre and the *recherché*, providing an opportunity for the author to display his erudition and indulge to the full his delight in the exotic. Wilde's verse had always worn its learning conspicuously. However, in early poems such as 'The Burden of Itys' (like 'The Garden of Eros' an Oxford Pastoral) this would sometimes impede the argument or narrative. The, at times somewhat formulaic and overwrought, Classical conceits and extended Homeric similes would often detract from the poem's meaning or effect. But with *The Sphinx* what was once an impediment becomes a positive advantage. Here digression and are ends in themselves. The digressive style of this later poem perfectly conforms with the context or situation of the poem – the overheated reveries of a somewhat precocious undergraduate. His obsessions are hatched from and coloured by his learning, enveloping his object in an aura of mythological and mystical association. The form of the poem is also appropriate to its subject, and to Wilde's particular genius. The longer lines, with their internal rhymes and cadences, suit perfectly the more fluid and 'rhetorical' demands of this particular poem. They are also closer to the patterns of that art which Wilde perhaps perfected above all others – speech:

> With Syrian oils his brows were bright: and widespread as
> a tent at noon
> His marble limbs made pearl the moon and lent the day a
> larger light.
>
> His long hair was nine cubits' span and coloured like that
> yellow gem

> Which hidden in their garment's hem the merchants bring
> from Kurdistan.

The same fanciful delight in language, its colours and its cadences, is found in so many of Wilde's works, from the fairy tales of *A House of Pomegranates* (1891), to the rich prose poetry of his play *Salomé* (1893–4), and the poetic prose of his criticism. Wilde's verse should not therefore be dismissed as an adjunct to the main body of his *oeuvre*. It provided him with a medium for experimentation with thought, form and language, and allowed him to perfect that which graces his finest work – poetry. It also provides the reader with valuable insights into Wilde's development as an artist and the evolution of his aesthetic.

The following selection emphasises this development. Its arrangement loosely conforms to the different phases of Wilde's poetic output. The first phase, which includes his 'political' poems and his 'devotional' pieces, as well as the long pastorals prepared for the first volume of *Poems*, finds Wilde at his most Romantic. Following these poems are found those which display Wilde the Aesthete, experimenting in the 'Impressionistic' and 'Symbolist' modes. The poems within this section were mostly published between 1882 and 1894, and are arranged chronologically by their date of publication.

The last poem included in the selection is perhaps Wilde's most famous. Whether its directness and relative simplicity, its didactic approach and its appeal to personal experience as an authority for art, suggest that Wilde's art was passing into a new phase, is open to speculation. Wilde's final and perhaps greatest poem was also his last work of art. In November 1900 the 'Infamous' St Oscar died, prophesying that he would become a martyr, and reminding us that he was also a poet.

ROBERT MIGHALL

Note On The Text

The policy of this edition is, wherever possible, to provide the most authoritative version of each text. This means the last version to be overseen by Wilde. Or, in the case of undated poems which remained unpublished during Wilde's lifetime, the fullest version, or the version which was, in the editor's view, the last to leave the author's hands. For poems from the first volume of *Poems*, published in 1881, I have used the 1882 edition, as these were often amended slightly by Wilde. For those pieces not included in this edition, or published after 1881, I have consulted the original texts rather than the ones found in Robert Ross's 'Collected' editions of 1908 and 1909. The few exceptions to this policy are indicated in the notes at the end of the selection. The text for *The Sphinx* is taken from the first edition, published by John Lane in 1894. However, as this edition is printed entirely in capitals, I have consulted the manuscript version of the poem held by the British Library for guidance.

In addition, there are a few poems which are taken from 'manuscript' sources, including 'O Golden Queen of life and joy', 'Desespoir', 'Pan: Double Villanelle' and 'La Circassienne'. These are taken from transcriptions of manuscripts which remained unpublished during Wilde's lifetime. These copies were made in 1908 by Walter Ledger, friend of Robert Ross and Stuart Mason who were working on the Collected Edition of Wilde's works at this time. These transcripts belong to the Robert Ross Memorial Collection held by the Bodleian Library, Oxford (Ross. MS. 9). The original manuscripts belonged to Robert Ross and were copied by Christopher Millard (Stuart Mason), and then Ledger made his own copies. Millard's copies of two of these poems ('O Golden Queen' and 'Desespoir') are found in the William Andrews Clark Library, Los Angeles (Finzi 2491). For the present edition, the texts for the four poems taken from Ledger's copies have not been ammended in any way. Exceptions to this rule and details about these poems are found in the notes at the end of the selection.

Oscar Wilde

Hélas!

To drift with every passion till my soul
Is a stringed lute on which all winds can play,
Is it for this that I have given away
Mine ancient wisdom, and austere control?
Methinks my life is a twice-written scroll
Scrawled over on some boyish holiday
With idle songs for pipe and virelay,
Which do but mar the secret of the whole.
Surely there was a time I might have trod
The sunlit heights, and from life's dissonance
Struck one clear chord to reach the ears of God:
Is that time dead? lo! with a little rod
I did but touch the honey of romance—
And must I lose a soul's inheritance?

Sonnet to Liberty

Not that I love thy children, whose dull eyes
See nothing save their own unlovely woe,
Whose minds know nothing, nothing care to know,—
But that the roar of thy Democracies,
Thy reigns of Terror, thy great Anarchies,
Mirror my wildest passions like the sea
And give my rage a brother –! Liberty!
For this sake only do thy dissonant cries
Delight my discreet soul, else might all kings
By bloody knout or treacherous cannonades
Rob nations of their rights inviolate
And I remain unmoved – and yet, and yet,
These Christs that die upon the barricades,
God knows it I am with them, in some things.

Theoretikos

This mighty empire hath but feet of clay:
    Of all its ancient chivalry and might
    Our little island is forsaken quite:
Some enemy hath stolen its crown of bay,
And from its hills that voice hath passed away
    Which spake of Freedom: O come out of it,
    Come out of it, my Soul, thou art not fit
For this vile traffic-house, where day by day
    Wisdom and reverence are sold at mart,
    And the rude people rage with ignorant cries
Against an heritage of centuries.
    It mars my calm: wherefore in dreams of Art
    And loftiest culture I would stand apart,
Neither for God, nor for his enemies.

Requiescat

Tread lightly, she is near
    Under the snow,
Speak gently, she can hear
    The daisies grow.

All her bright golden hair
    Tarnished with rust,
She that was young and fair
    Fallen to dust.

Lily-like, white as snow,
    She hardly knew
She was a woman, so
    Sweetly she grew.

Coffin-board, heavy stone,
    Lie on her breast,

I vex my heart alone,
    She is at rest.

Peace, Peace, she cannot hear
    Lyre or sonnet,
All my life's buried here,
    Heap earth upon it.

San Miniato

See, I have climbed the mountain side
Up to this holy house of God,
Where once that Angel-Painter trod
Who saw the heavens opened wide,

And throned upon the crescent moon
The Virginal white Queen of Grace,—
Mary! could I but see thy face
Death could not come at all too soon.

O crowned by God with thorns and pain!
Mother of Christ! O mystic wife!
My heart is weary of this life
And over-sad to sing again.

O crowned by God with love and flame!
O crowned by Christ the Holy One!
O listen ere the searching sun
Show to the world my sin and shame.

Sonnet

On hearing the *Dies Iræ* sung in the Sistine Chapel

Nay, Lord, not thus! white lilies in the spring,
 Sad olive-groves, or silver-breasted dove,
 Teach me more clearly of Thy life and love
Than terrors of red flame and thundering.
The hillside vines dear memories of Thee bring:
 A bird at evening flying to its nest
 Tells me of One who had no place of rest:
I think it is of Thee the sparrows sing.
Come rather on some autumn afternoon,
 When red and brown are burnished on the leaves,
 And the fields echo to the gleaner's song,
Come when the splendid fulness of the moon
 Looks down upon the rows of golden sheaves,
 And reap Thy harvest: we have waited long.

Ave Maria Plena Gratia

Was this His coming! I had hoped to see
 A scene of wondrous glory, as was told
 Of some great God who in a rain of gold
Broke open bars and fell on Danae:
Or a dread vision as when Semele
 Sickening for love and unappeased desire
 Prayed to see God's clear body, and the fire
Caught her brown limbs and slew her utterly:
With such glad dreams I sought this holy place,
 And now with wondering eyes and heart I stand
 Before this supreme mystery of Love:
Some kneeling girl with passionless pale face,
 An angel with a lily in his hand,
 And over both the white wings of a Dove.

Madonna Mia

A lily-girl, not made for this world's pain,
   With brown, soft hair close braided by her ears,
   And longing eyes half veiled by slumberous tears
Like bluest water seen through mists of rain:
Pale cheeks whereon no love hath left its stain,
   Red underlip drawn in for fear of love,
   And white throat, whiter than the silvered dove,
Through whose wan marble creeps one purple vein.
Yet, though my lips shall praise her without cease,
   Even to kiss her feet I am not bold,
   Being o'ershadowed by the wings of awe.
Like Dante, when he stood with Beatrice
   Beneath the flaming Lion's breast, and saw
   The seventh Crystal, and the Stair of Gold.

Untitled

O Golden Queen of life and joy!
  O Lily without blot or stain!
O Loved as only loves a boy!
  O Loved in vain! O Loved in vain!

Ah, what to thee is war or peace,
  Who holdest all the keys of life,
Though the white fleets of gold should cease,
  And the blue seas be vexed with strife!

Bring poppy flower and poppy root,
  And yellow-petaled mandragore,
Bring berries of that purple fruit
  Which sleeps on Ocean's sleepless shore.

And when remorse and ruin come,
  And the glad pulse of youth is low,
O Helen! Helen! mingle some
  Divine nepenthe for my woe.

Till o'er the flower-foamed fields of sea
  On violet wing night steals away,
And God's white fingers open wide
  The crimson lips of risen day.

Tristitiæ

O well for him who lives at ease
  With garned gold in wide domain!
  Nor heeds the splashing of the rain,
The crashing down of forest trees.

O well for him who ne'er hath known
  The travail of the hungry years,
  A father grey with grief and tears,
A mother weeping all alone.

But well for him whose feet have trod
  The weary road of earthly strife,
  Yet from the sorrows of his life
Builds ladders to be nearer God.

Desespoir

The seasons mend their ruin as they go,
For in the spring the narciss shows its head
Nor withers till the rose has flamed to red,
And in the autumn purple violets blow,
And the slim crocus stirs the winter snow;
Wherefore yon leafless trees will bloom again
And this grey land grow green with summer rain
And send up cowslips for some boy to mow.
But what of life whose bitter hungry sea
Flows at our heels, and gloom of sunless night
Covers the days which never more return?
Ambition, love and all the thoughts that burn
We lose too soon, and only find delight
In withered husks of some dead memory.

The Grave of Keats

Rid of the world's injustice, and his pain,
    He rests at last beneath God's veil of blue:
    Taken from life when life and love were new
The youngest of the martyrs here is lain,
Fair as Sebastian, and as early slain.
    No cypress shades his grave or funeral yew,
    But gentle violets weeping with the dew
Weave on his bones an everblossoming chain.
O proudest heart that broke for misery!
    O sweetest lips since those of Mitylene!
    O poet-painter of our English Land!
Thy name was writ in water – it shall stand:
    And tears like mine shall keep thy memory green,
    As Isabella did her Basil-Tree.

Magdalen Walks

The little white clouds are racing over the sky,
   And the fields are strewn with the gold of the flower of March,
   The daffodil breaks under foot, and the tasselled larch
Sways and swings as the thrush goes hurrying by.

A delicate odour is borne on the wings of the morning breeze,
   The odour of deep wet grass, and of brown new-furrowed
      earth,
   The birds are singing for joy of the Spring's glad birth,
Hopping from branch to branch on the rocking trees.

And all the woods are alive with the murmur and sound of
      Spring,
   And the rosebud breaks into pink on the climbing briar,
   And the crocus-bed is a quivering moon of fire
Girdled round with the belt of an amethyst ring.

And the plane to the pine-tree is whispering some tale of love
   Till it rustles with laughter and tosses its mantle of green,
   And the gloom of the wych-elm's hollow is lit with the iris
      sheen
Of the burnished rainbow throat and the silver breast of a dove.

See! the lark starts up from his bed in the meadow there,
   Breaking the gossamer threads and the nets of dew,
   And flashing a-down the river, a flame of blue!
The kingfisher flies like an arrow, and wounds the air.

Chanson

A ring of gold and a milk-white dove
   Are goodly gifts for thee,
And a hempen rope for your own love
   To hang upon a tree.

For you a House of Ivory
   (Roses are white in the rose-bower)!
A narrow bed for me to lie
   (White, O white, is the hemlock flower)!

Myrtle and jessamine for you
   (O the red rose is fair to see)!
For me the cypress and the rue
   (Fairest of all is rose-mary)!

For you three lovers of your hand
   (Green grass where a man lies dead)!
For me three paces on the sand
   (Plant lilies at my head)!

Pan: Double Villanelle

I

O GOAT-FOOT GOD of Arcady!
   This modern world is grey and old,
And what remains to us of thee?

No more the shepherd lads in glee
   Throw apples at thy wattled fold.
O goat-foot God of Arcady!

Nor through the laurels can one see
   Thy soft brown limbs, thy beard of gold,
And what remains to us of thee?

And dull and dead our Thames would be   10
   For here the winds are chill and cold,
O goat-foot God of Arcady!

Then keep the tomb of Helicé,
   Thine olive-woods, thy vine-clad wold,
And what remains to us of thee?

Though many an unsung elegy
   Sleeps in the reeds our rivers hold,
O goat-foot God of Arcady!
Ah, what remains to us of thee?

II

AH, leave the hills of Arcady,   20
   Thy satyrs and their wanton play,
This modern world hath need of thee.

No nymph or Faun indeed have we,
   For Faun and nymph are old and grey,
Ah, leave the hills of Arcady!

This is the land where Liberty
   Lit grave-browed Milton on his way,
This modern world hath need of thee!

A land of ancient chivalry
   Where gentle Sidney saw the day,   30
Ah, leave the hills of Arcady!

This fierce sea-lion of the sea,
   This England, lacks some stronger lay,
This modern world hath need of thee!

Then blow some trumpet loud and free,
   And give thine oaten pipe away,
Ah, leave the hills of Arcady!
This modern world hath need of thee!

from The Garden of Eros

It is full summer now, the heart of June,
    Not yet the sun-burnt reapers are a-stir
Upon the upland meadow where too soon
    Rich autumn time, the season's usurer,
Will lend his hoarded gold to all the trees,
And see his treasure scattered by the wild and spend-thrift
    breeze.

Too soon indeed! yet here the daffodil,
    That love-child of the Spring, has lingered on
To vex the rose with jealousy, and still
    The harebell spreads her azure pavilion,   10
And like a strayed and wandering reveller
Abandoned of its brothers, whom long since June's
    messenger

The missel-thrush has frighted from the glade,
    One pale narcissus loiters fearfully
Close to a shadowy nook, where half afraid
    Of their own loveliness some violets lie
That will not look the gold sun in the face
For fear of too much splendour, – ah! methinks it is a place

Which should be trodden by Persephone
    When wearied of the flowerless fields of Dis!   20
Or danced on by the lads of Arcady!
    The hidden secret of eternal bliss
Known to the Grecian here a man might find,
Ah! you and I may find it now if Love and Sleep be kind.

                    *   *   *

Spirit of Beauty! tarry still a-while,
    They are not dead, thine ancient votaries,
Some few there are to whom thy radiant smile
    Is better than a thousand victories,
Though all the nobly slain of Waterloo
Rise up in wrath against them! tarry still, there are a few

Who for thy sake would give their manlihood
   And consecrate their being, I at least   110
Have done so, made thy lips my daily food,
   And in thy temples found a goodlier feast
Than this starved age can give me, spite of all
Its new-found creeds so sceptical and so dogmatical.

Here not Cephissos, not Ilissos flows,
   The woods of white Colonos are not here,
On our bleak hills the olive never blows,
   No simple priest conducts his lowing steer
Up the steep marble way, nor through the town
Do laughing maidens bear to thee the crocus-flowered
     gown.   120

Yet tarry! for the boy who loved thee best,
   Whose very name should be a memory
To make thee linger, sleeps in silent rest
   Beneath the Roman walls, and melody
Still mourns her sweetest lyre, none can play
The lute of Adonais, with his lips Song passed away.

Nay, when Keats died the Muses still had left
   One silver voice to sing his threnody,
But ah! too soon of it we were bereft
   When on that riven night and stormy sea   130
Panthea claimed her singer as her own,
And slew the mouth that praised her; since which time we
   walk alone,

Save for that fiery heart, that morning star
   Of re-arisen England, whose clear eye
Saw from our tottering throne and waste of war
   The grand Greek limbs of young Democracy
Rise mightily like Hesperus and bring
The great Republic! him at least thy love hath taught to
   sing,

And he hath been with thee at Thessaly,
   And seen white Atalanta fleet of foot   140

In passionless and fierce virginity
    Hunting the tuskéd boar, his honied lute
Hath pierced the cavern of the hollow hill,
And Venus laughs to know one knee will bow before her
    still.

And he hath kissed the lips of Proserpine,
    And sung the Galilæan's requiem,
That wounded forehead dashed with blood and wine
    He hath discrowned, the Ancient Gods in him
Have found their last, most ardent worshipper,
And the new Sign grows grey and dim before its conqueror.   150

Spirit of Beauty! tarry with us still,
    It is not quenched the torch of poesy,
The star that shook above the Eastern hill
    Holds unassailed its argent armoury
From all the gathering gloom and fretful fight—
O tarry with us still! for through the long and common
    night,

Morris, our sweet and simple Chaucer's child,
    Dear heritor of Spenser's tuneful reed,
With soft and sylvan pipe has oft beguiled
    The weary soul of man in troublous need,   160
And from the far and flowerless fields of ice
Has brought fair flowers meet to make an earthly paradise.

We know them all, Gudrun the strong men's bride,
    Aslaug and Olafson we know them all,
How giant Grettir fought and Sigurd died,
    And what enchantment held the king in thrall
When lonely Brynhild wrestled with the powers
That war against all passion, ah! how oft through summer
    hours,

Long listless summer hours when the noon
    Being enamoured of a damask rose   170
Forgets to journey westward, till the moon

The pale usurper of its tribute grows
From a thin sickle to a silver shield
And chides its loitering car – how oft, in some cool grassy
    field

Far from the cricket-ground and noisy eight,
    At Bagley, where the rustling bluebells come
Almost before the blackbird finds a mate
    And overstay the swallow, and the hum
Of many murmuring bees flits through the leaves,
Have I lain poring on the dreamy tales his fancy weaves,   180

And through their unreal woes and mimic pain
    Wept for myself, and so was purified,
And in their simple mirth grew glad again;
    For as I sailed upon that pictured tide
The strength and splendour of the storm was mine
Without the storm's red ruin, for the singer is divine,

The little laugh of water falling down
    Is not so musical, the clammy gold
Close hoarded in the tiny waxen town
    Has less of sweetness in it, and the old   190
Half-withered reeds that waved in Arcady
Touched by his lips break forth again to fresher harmony.

Spirit of Beauty tarry yet a-while!
    Although the cheating merchants of the mart
With iron roads profane our lovely isle,
    And break on whirling wheels the limbs of Art,
Ay! though the crowded factories beget
The blind-worm Ignorance that slays the soul, O tarry yet!

For One at least there is, – He bears his name
    From Dante and the seraph Gabriel,—   200
Whose double laurels burn with deathless flame
    To light thine altar; He too loves thee well,
Who saw old Merlin lured in Vivien's snare,
And the white feet of angels coming down the golden stair,

Loves thee so well, that all the World for him
   A gorgeous-coloured vestiture must wear,
And Sorrow take a purple diadem,
   Or else be no more Sorrow, and Despair
Gild its own thorns, and Pain, like Adon, be
Even in anguish beautiful; – such is the empery   210

Which Painters hold, and such the heritage
   This gentle solemn Spirit doth possess,
Being a better mirror of his age
   In all his pity, love, and weariness,
Than those who can but copy common things,
And leave the Soul unpainted with its mighty questionings.

But they are few, and all romance has flown,
   And men can prophesy about the sun,
And lecture on his arrows – how, alone,
   Through a waste void the soulless atoms run,   220
How from each tree its weeping nymph has fled,
And that no more 'mid English reeds a Naïad shows her
   head.

Methinks these new Actæons boast too soon
   That they have spied on beauty; what if we
Have analyzed the rainbow, robbed the moon
   Of her most ancient, chastest mystery,
Shall I, the last Endymion, lose all hope
Because rude eyes peer at my mistress through a telescope!

What profit if this scientific age
   Burst through our gates with all its retinue   230
Of modern miracles! Can it assuage
   One lover's breaking heart? what can it do
To make one life more beautiful, one day
More god-like in its period? but now the Age of Clay

Returns in horrid cycle, and the earth
   Hath borne again a noisy progeny
Of ignorant Titans, whose ungodly birth

Hurls them against the august hierarchy
Which sat upon Olympus, to the Dust
They have appealed, and to that barren arbiter they must   240

Repair for judgment, let them, if they can,
    From Natural Warfare and insensate Chance,
Create the new Ideal rule for man!
    Methinks that was not my inheritance;
For I was nurtured otherwise, my soul
Passes from higher heights of life to a more supreme goal.

Lo! while we spake the earth did turn away
    Her visage from the God, and Hecate's boat
Rose silver-laden, till the jealous day
    Blew all its torches out: I did not note   250
The waning hours, to young Endymions
Time's palsied fingers count in vain his rosary of suns!

Mark how the yellow iris wearily
    Leans back its throat, as though it would be kissed
By its false chamberer, the dragon-fly,
    Who, like a blue vein on a girl's white wrist,
Sleeps on that snowy primrose of the night,
Which 'gins to flush with crimson shame, and die beneath
    the light.

Come let us go, against the pallid shield
    Of the wan sky the almond blossoms gleam,   260
The corn-crake nested in the unmown field
    Answers its mate, across the misty stream
On fitful wing the startled curlews fly,
And in his sedgy bed the lark, for joy that Day is nigh,

Scatters the pearléd dew from off the grass,
    In tremulous ecstasy to greet the sun,
Who soon in gilded panoply will pass
    Forth from yon orange-curtained pavilion
Hung in the burning east, see, the red rim
O'ertops the expectant hills! it is the God! for love of him   270

Already the shrill lark is out of sight,
   Flooding with waves of song this silent dell,—
Ah! there is something more in that bird's flight
   Than could be tested in a crucible!—
But the air freshens, let us go, why soon
The woodmen will be here; how we have lived this night of
   June!

La Bella Donna Della Mia Mente

My limbs are wasted with a flame,
   My feet are sore with travelling,
For calling on my Lady's name
   My lips have now forgot to sing.

O Linnet in the wild-rose brake
   Strain for my Love thy melody,
O Lark sing louder for love's sake,
   My gentle Lady passeth by.

She is too fair for any man
   To see or hold his heart's delight,   10
Fairer than Queen or courtezan
   Or moon-lit water in the night.

Her hair is bound with myrtle leaves,
   (Green leaves upon her golden hair!)
Green grasses through the yellow sheaves
   Of autumn corn are not more fair.

Her little lips, more made to kiss
   Than to cry bitterly for pain,
Are tremulous as brook-water is,
   Or roses after evening rain.   20

Her neck is like white melilote
   Flushing for pleasure of the sun,

The throbbing of the linnet's throat
  Is not so sweet to look upon.

As a pomegranate, cut in twain,
  White-seeded, is her crimson mouth,
Her cheeks are as the fading stain
  Where the peach reddens to the south.

O twining hands! O delicate
  White body made for love and pain!
O House of love! O desolate
  Pale flower beaten by the rain!

                30

By The Arno

The oleander on the wall
  Grows crimson in the dawning light,
  Though the grey shadows of the night
Lie yet on Florence like a pall.

The dew is bright upon the hill,
  And bright the blossoms overhead,
  But ah! the grasshoppers have fled,
The little Attic song is still.

Only the leaves are gently stirred
  By the soft breathing of the gale,
  And in the almond-scented vale
The lonely nightingale is heard.

                10

The day will make thee silent soon,
  O nightingale sing on for love!
  While yet upon the shadowy grove
Splinter the arrows of the moon.

Before across the silent lawn
In sea-green vest the morning steals,
And to love's frightened eyes reveals
The long white fingers of the dawn 20

Fast climbing up the eastern sky
To grasp and slay the shuddering night,
All careless of my heart's delight,
Or if the nightingale should die.

Charmides

I

He was a Grecian lad, who coming home
  With pulpy figs and wine from Sicily
Stood at his galley's prow, and let the foam
  Blow through his crisp brown curls unconsciously,
And holding wave and wind in boy's despite
Peered from his dripping seat across the wet and stormy
    night

Till with the dawn he saw a burnished spear
  Like a thin thread of gold against the sky,
And hoisted sail, and strained the creaking gear,
  And bade the pilot head her lustily 10
Against the nor'west gale, and all day long
Held on his way, and marked the rowers' time with
    measured song,

And when the faint Corinthian hills were red
  Dropped anchor in a little sandy bay,
And with fresh boughs of olive crowned his head,
  And brushed from cheek and throat the hoary spray,
And washed his limbs with oil, and from the hold
Brought out his linen tunic and his sandals brazen-soled,

And a rich robe stained with the fishes' juice
   Which of some swarthy trader he had bought   20
Upon the sunny quay at Syracuse,
   And was with Tyrian broideries inwrought,
And by the questioning merchants made his way
Up through the soft and silver woods, and when the
   labouring day

Had spun its tangled web of crimson cloud,
   Clomb the high hill, and with swift silent feet
Crept to the fane unnoticed by the crowd
   Of busy priests, and from some dark retreat
Watched the young swains his frolic playmates bring
The firstling of their little flock, and the shy shepherd fling   30

The crackling salt upon the flame, or hang
   His studded crook against the temple wall
To Her who keeps away the ravenous fang
   Of the base wolf from homestead and from stall;
And then the clear-voiced maidens 'gan to sing,
And to the altar each man brought some goodly offering,

A beechen cup brimming with milky foam,
   A fair cloth wrought with cunning imagery
Of hounds in chase, a waxen honey-comb
   Dripping with oozy gold which scarce the bee   40
Had ceased from building, a black skin of oil
Meet for the wrestlers, a great boar the fierce and white-
   tusked spoil

Stolen from Artemis that jealous maid
   To please Athena, and the dappled hide
Of a tall stag who in some mountain glade
   Had met the shaft; and then the herald cried,
And from the pillared precinct one by one
Went the glad Greeks well pleased that they their simple
   vows had done.

And the old priest put out the waning fires
   Save that one lamp whose restless ruby glowed   50

For ever in the cell, and the shrill lyres
   Came fainter on the wind, as down the road
In joyous dance these country folk did pass,
And with stout hands the warder closed the gates of
   polished brass.

Long time he lay and hardly dared to breathe,
   And heard the cadenced drip of spilt-out wine,
And the rose-petals falling from the wreath
   As the night breezes wandered through the shrine,
And seemed to be in some entrancèd swoon
Till through the open roof above the full and brimming
   moon   60

Flooded with sheeny waves the marble floor,
   When from his nook upleapt the venturous lad,
And flinging wide the cedar-carven door
   Beheld an awful image saffron-clad
And armed for battle! the gaunt Griffin glared
From the huge helm, and the long lance of wreck and ruin
   flared

Like a red rod of flame, stony and steeled
   The Gorgon's head its leaden eyeballs rolled,
And writhed its snaky horrors through the shield,
   And gaped aghast with bloodless lips and cold   70
In passion impotent, while with blind gaze
The blinking owl between the feet hooted in shrill amaze.

The lonely fisher as he trimmed his lamp
   Far out at sea off Sunium, or cast
The net for tunnies, heard a brazen tramp
   Of horses smite the waves, and a wild blast
Divide the folded curtains of the night,
And knelt upon the little poop, and prayed in holy fright.

And guilty lovers in their venery
   Forgat a little while their stolen sweets,   80
Deeming they heard dread Dian's bitter cry;
   And the grim watchmen on their lofty seats

Ran to their shields in haste precipitate,
Or strained black-bearded throats across the dusky parapet.

For round the temple rolled the clang of arms,
   And the twelve Gods leapt up in marble fear,
And the air quaked with dissonant alarums
   Till huge Poseidon shook his mighty spear,
And on the frieze the prancing horses neighed,
And the low tread of hurrying feet rang from the cavalcade.   90

Ready for death with parted lips he stood,
   And well content at such a price to see
That calm wide brow, that terrible maidenhood,
   The marvel of that pitiless chastity,
Ah! well content indeed, for never wight
Since Troy's young shepherd prince had seen so wonderful
   a sight.

Ready for death he stood, but lo! the air
   Grew silent, and the horses ceased to neigh,
And off his brow he tossed the clustering hair,
   And from his limbs he threw the cloak away,   100
For whom would not such love make desperate,
And nigher came, and touched her throat, and with hands
   violate

Undid the cuirass, and the crocus gown,
   And bared the breasts of polished ivory,
Till from the waist the peplos falling down
   Left visible the secret mystery
Which to no lover will Athena show,
The grand cool flanks, the crescent thighs, the bossy hills of
   snow.

A little space he let his greedy eyes
   Rest on the burnished image, till mere sight   110
Half swooned for surfeit of such luxuries,
   And then his lips in hungering delight
Fed on her lips, and round the towered neck

He flung his arms, nor cared at all his passion's will to
  check.

Never I ween did lover hold such tryst,
  For all night long he murmured honeyed word,
And saw her sweet unravished limbs, and kissed
  Her pale and argent body undisturbed,
And paddled with the polished throat, and pressed
His hot and beating heart upon her chill and icy breast.   120

It was as if Numidian javelins
  Pierced through and through his wild and whirling
    brain,
And his nerves thrilled like throbbing violins
  In exquisite pulsation, and the pain
Was such sweet anguish that he never drew
His lips from hers till overhead the lark of warning flew.

The moon was girdled with a crystal rim,
  The sign which shipmen say is ominous
Of wrath in heaven, the wan stars were dim,
  And the low lightening east was tremulous   130
With the faint fluttering wings of flying dawn,
Ere from the silent sombre shrine this lover had withdrawn.

Down the steep rock with hurried feet and fast
  Clomb the brave lad, and reached the cave of Pan,
And heard the goat-foot snoring as he passed,
  And leapt upon a grassy knoll and ran
Like a young fawn unto an olive wood
Which in a shady valley by the well-built city stood.

And sought a little stream, which well he knew,
  For oftentimes with boyish careless shout   140
The green and crested grebe he would pursue,
  Or snare in woven net the silver trout,
And down amid the startled reeds he lay
Panting in breathless sweet affright, and waited for the day.

On the green bank he lay, and let one hand
  Dip in the cool dark eddies listlessly,

And soon the breath of morning came and fanned
  His hot flushed cheeks, or lifted wantonly
The tangled curls from off his forehead, while
He on the running water gazed with strange and secret
  smile.   150

And soon the shepherd in rough woollen cloak
  With his long crook undid the wattled cotes,
And from the stack a thin blue wreath of smoke
  Curled through the air across the ripening oats,
And on the hill the yellow house-dog bayed
As through the crisp and rustling fern the heavy cattle
  strayed.

And when the light-foot mower went afield
  Across the meadows laced with threaded dew,
And the sheep bleated on the misty weald,
  And from its nest the waking corn-crake flew,   160
Some woodmen saw him lying by the stream
And marvelled much that any lad so beautiful could seem,

Nor deemed him born of mortals, and one said,
  'It is young Hylas, that false runaway
Who with a Naïad now would make his bed
  Forgetting Herakles,' but others, 'Nay,
It is Narcissus, his own paramour,
Those are the fond and crimson lips no woman can allure.'

And when they nearer came a third one cried,
  'It is young Dionysos who has hid   170
His spear and fawnskin by the river side
  Weary of hunting with the Bassarid,
And wise indeed were we away to fly
They live not long who on the gods immortal come to spy.'

So turned they back, and feared to look behind,
  And told the timid swain how they had seen
Amid the reeds some woodland God reclined,
  And no man dared to cross the open green,

And on that day no olive-tree was slain,
Nor rushes cut, but all deserted was the fair domain.   180

Save when the neat-herd's lad, his empty pail
    Well slung upon his back, with leap and bound
Raced on the other side, and stopped to hail
    Hoping that he some comrade new had found,
And gat no answer, and then half afraid
Passed on his simple way, or down the still and silent glade

A little girl ran laughing from the farm
    Not thinking of love's secret mysteries,
And when she saw the white and gleaming arm
    And all his manlihood, with longing eyes   190
Whose passion mocked her sweet virginity
Watched him a-while, and then stole back sadly and
    wearily.

Far off he heard the city's hum and noise,
    And now and then the shriller laughter where
The passionate purity of brown-limbed boys
    Wrestled or raced in the clear healthful air,
And now and then a little tinkling bell
As the shorn wether led the sheep down to the mossy well.

Through the grey willows danced the fretful gnat,
    The grasshopper chirped idly from the tree,   200
In sleek and oily coat the water-rat
    Breasting the little ripples manfully
Made for the wild-duck's nest, from bough to bough
Hopped the shy finch, and the huge tortoise crept across the
    slough.

On the faint wind floated the silky seeds
    As the bright scythe swept through the waving grass,
The ousel-cock splashed circles in the reeds
    And flecked with silver whorls the forest's glass,
Which scare had caught again its imagery
Ere from its bed the dusky tench leapt at the dragon-fly.   210

But little care had he for any thing
    Though up and down the beech the squirrel played,

And from the copse the linnet 'gan to sing
    To her brown mate her sweetest serenade,
Ah! little care indeed, for he had seen
The breasts of Pallas and the naked wonder of the Queen.

But when the herdsman called his straggling goats
    With whistling pipe across the rocky road,
And the shard-beetle with its trumpet-notes
    Boomed through the darkening woods, and seemed to
        bode   220
Of coming storm, and the belated crane
Passed homeward like a shadow, and the dull big drops of
    rain

Fell on the pattering fig-leaves, up he rose,
    And from the gloomy forest went his way
Past sombre homestead and wet orchard-close,
    And came at last unto a little quay,
And called his mates a-board, and took his seat
On the high poop, and pushed from land, and loosed the
    dripping sheet,

And steered across the bay, and when nine suns
    Passed down the long and laddered way of gold,   230
And nine pale moons had breathed their orisons
    To the chaste stars their confessors, or told
Their dearest secret to the downy moth
That will not fly at noonday, through the foam and surging
    froth

Came a great owl with yellow sulphurous eyes
    And lit upon the ship, whose timbers creaked
As though the lading of three argosies
    Were in the hold, and flapped its wings, and shrieked,
And darkness straightway stole across the deep,
Sheathed was Orion's sword, dread Mars himself fled down
    the steep,   240

And the moon hid behind a tawny mask
    Of drifting cloud, and from the ocean's marge

Rose the red plume, the huge and hornèd casque,
    The seven-cubit spear, the brazen targe!
And clad in bright and burnished panoply
Athena strode across the stretch of sick and shivering sea!

To the dull sailors' sight her loosened locks
    Seemed like the jagged storm-rack, and her feet
Only the spume that floats on hidden rocks,
    And, marking how the rising waters beat   250
Against the rolling ship, the pilot cried
To the young helmsman at the stern to luff to windward
    side.

But he, the over-bold adulterer,
    A dear profaner of great mysteries,
An ardent amorous idolater,
    When he beheld those grand relentless eyes
Laughed loud for joy, and crying out 'I come'
Leapt from the lofty poop into the chill and churning foam.

Then fell from the high heaven one bright star,
    One dancer left the circling galaxy,   260
And back to Athens on her clattering car
    In all the pride of venged divinity
Pale Pallas swept with shrill and steely clank,
And a few gurgling bubbles rose where her boy lover sank.

And the mast shuddered as the gaunt owl flew
    With mocking hoots after the wrathful Queen,
And the old pilot bade the trembling crew
    Hoist the big sail, and told how he had seen
Close to the stern a dim and giant form,
And like a dipping swallow the stout ship dashed through
    the storm.   270

And no man dared to speak of Charmides
    Deeming that he some evil thing had wrought,
And when they reached the strait Symplegades
    They beached their galley on the shore, and sought

The toll-gate of the city hastily,
And in the market showed their brown and pictured
    pottery.

II

But some good Triton-god had ruth, and bare
    The boy's drowned body back to Grecian land,
And mermaids combed his dank and dripping hair
    And smoothed his brow, and loosed his clenching hand,   280
Some brought sweet spices from far Araby,
And others bade the halcyon sing her softest lullaby.

And when he neared his old Athenian home,
    A mighty billow rose up suddenly
Upon whose oily back the clotted foam
    Lay diapered in some strange fantasy,
And clasping him unto its glassy breast,
Swept landward, like a white-maned steed upon a
    venturous quest!

Now where Colonos leans unto the sea
    There lies a long and level stretch of lawn,   290
The rabbit knows it, and the mountain bee
    For it deserts Hymettus, and the Faun
Is not afraid, for never through the day
Comes a cry ruder than the shout of shepherd lads at play.

But often from the thorny labyrinth
    And tangled branches of the circling wood
The stealthy hunter sees young Hyacinth
    Hurling the polished disk, and draws his hood
Over his guilty gaze, and creeps away,
Nor dares to wind his horn, or – else at the first break of day   300

The Dryads come and throw the leathern ball
    Along the reedy shore, and circumvent
Some goat-eared Pan to be their seneschal
    For fear of bold Poseidon's ravishment,
And loose their girdles, with shy timorous eyes,
Lest from the surf his azure arms and purple beard should
    rise.

On this side and on that a rocky cave,
    Hung with the yellow-bell'd laburnum, stands,
Smooth is the beach, save where some ebbing wave
    Leaves its faint outline etched upon the sands,   310
As though it feared to be too soon forgot
By the green rush, its playfellow, – and yet, it is a spot

So small, that the inconstant butterfly
    Could steal the hoarded honey from each flower
Ere it was noon, and still not satisfy
    Its over-greedy love, – within an hour
A sailor boy, were he but rude enow
To land and pluck a garland for his galley's painted prow,

Would almost leave the little meadow bare,
    For it knows nothing of great pageantry,   320
Only a few narcissi here and there
    Stand separate in sweet austerity,
Dotting the unmown grass with silver stars,
And here and there a daffodil waves tiny scimetars.

Hither the billow brought him, and was glad
    Of such dear servitude, and where the land
Was virgin of all waters laid the lad
    Upon the golden margent of the strand,
And like a lingering lover oft returned
To kiss those pallid limbs which once with intense fire
    burned,   330

Ere the wet seas had quenched that holocaust,
    That self-fed flame, that passionate lustihead,
Ere grisly death with chill and nipping frost
    Had withered up those lilies white and red
Which, while the boy would through the forest range,
Answered each other in a sweet antiphonal counter-
    change.

And when at dawn the woodnymphs, hand-in-hand,
    Threaded the bosky dell, their satyr spied

The boy's pale body stretched upon the sand,
   And feared Poseidon's treachery, and cried,   340
And like bright sunbeams flitting through a glade,
Each startled Dryad sought some safe and leafy ambuscade.

Save one white girl, who deemed it would not be
   So dread a thing to feel a sea-god's arms
Crushing her breasts in amorous tyranny,
   And longed to listen to those subtle charms
Insidious lovers weave when they would win
Some fencèd fortress, and stole back again, nor thought it
   sin

To yield her treasure unto one so fair,
   And lay beside him, thirsty with love's drouth,   350
Called him soft names, played with his tangled hair,
   And with hot lips made havoc of his mouth
Afraid he might not wake, and then afraid
Lest he might wake too soon, fled back, and then, fond
   renegade,

Returned to fresh assault, and all day long
   Sat at his side, and laughed at her new toy,
And held his hand, and sang her sweetest song,
   Then frowned to see how froward was the boy
Who would not with her maidenhood entwine,
Nor knew that three days since his eyes had looked on
   Proserpine,
                               360

Nor knew what sacrilege his lips had done,
   But said, 'He will awake, I know him well,
He will awake at evening when the sun
   Hangs his red shield on Corinth's citadel,
This sleep is but a cruel treachery
To make me love him more, and in some cavern of the sea

Deeper than ever falls the fisher's line
   Already a huge Triton blows his horn,
And weaves a garland from the crystalline

And drifting ocean-tendrils to adorn   370
The emerald pillars of our bridal bed,
For sphered in foaming silver, and with coral-crownèd
    head,

We two will sit upon a throne of pearl,
    And a blue wave will be our canopy,
And at our feet the water-snakes will curl
    In all their amethystine panoply
Of diamonded mail, and we will mark
The mullets swimming by the mast of some storm-
    foundered bark,

Vermilion-finned with eyes of bossy gold
    Like flakes of crimson light, and the great deep   380
His glassy-portaled chamber will unfold,
    And we will see the painted dolphins sleep
Cradled by murmuring halcyons on the rocks
Where Proteus in quaint suit of green pastures his
    monstrous flocks.

And tremulous opal-hued anemones
    Will wave their purple fringes where we tread
Upon the mirrored floor, and argosies
    Of fishes flecked with tawny scales will thread
The drifting cordage of the shattered wreck,
And honey-coloured amber beads our twining limbs will
    deck.'   390

But when that baffled Lord of War the Sun
    With gaudy pennon flying passed away
Into his brazen House, and one by one
    The little yellow stars began to stray
Across the field of heaven, ah! then indeed
She feared his lips upon her lips would never care to feed,

And cried, 'Awake, already the pale moon
    Washes the trees with silver, and the wave
Creeps grey and chilly up this sandy dune,
    The croaking frogs are out, and from the cave   400

The night-jar shrieks, the fluttering bats repass,
And the brown stoat with hollow flanks creeps through the
   dusky grass.

Nay, though thou art a God, be not so coy,
   For in yon stream there is a little reed
That often whispers how a lovely boy
   Lay with her once upon a grassy mead,
Who when his cruel pleasure he had done
Spread wings of rustling gold and soared aloft into the sun.

Be not so coy, the laurel trembles still
   With great Apollo's kisses, and the fir   410
Whose clustering sisters fringe the sea-ward hill
   Hath many a tale of that bold ravisher
Whom men call Boreas, and I have seen
The mocking eyes of Hermes through the poplar's silvery
   sheen.

Even the jealous Naiads call me fair,
   And every morn a young and ruddy swain
Woos me with apples and with locks of hair,
   And seeks to soothe my virginal disdain
By all the gifts the gentle wood-nymphs love;
But yesterday he brought to me an iris-plumaged dove   420

With little crimson feet, which with its store
   Of seven spotted eggs the cruel lad
Had stolen from the lofty sycamore
   At day-break, when her amorous comrade had
Flown off in search of berried juniper
Which most they love; the fretful wasp, that earliest
   vintager

Of the blue grapes, hath not persistency
   So constant as this simple shepherd-boy
For my poor lips, his joyous purity
   And laughing sunny eyes might well decoy   430
A Dryad from her oath to Artemis;
For very beautiful is he, his mouth was made to kiss,

His argent forehead, like a rising moon
   Over the dusky hills of meeting brows,
Is crescent shaped, the hot and Tyrian noon
   Leads from the myrtle-grove no goodlier spouse
For Cytheræa, the first silky down
Fringes his blushing cheeks, and his young limbs are strong
   and brown:

And he is rich, and fat and fleecy herds
   Of bleating sheep upon his meadows lie,   440
And many an earthern bowl of yellow curds
   Is in his homestead for the thievish fly
To swim and drown in, the pink clover mead
Keeps its sweet store for him, and he can pipe on oaten reed.

And yet I love him not, it was for thee
   I kept my love, I knew that thou would'st come
To rid me of this pallid chastity;
   Thou fairest flower of the flowerless foam
Of all the wide Ægean, brightest star
Of ocean's azure heavens where the mirrored planets are!   450

I knew that thou would'st come, for when at first
   The dry wood burgeoned, and the sap of Spring
Swelled in my green and tender bark or burst
   To myriad multitudinous blossoming
Which mocked the midnight with its mimic moons
That did not dread the dawn, and first the thrushes'
   rapturous tunes

Startled the squirrel from its granary,
   And cuckoo flowers fringed the narrow lane,
Through my young leaves a sensuous ecstasy
   Crept like new wine, and every mossy vein   460
Throbbed with the fitful pulse of amorous blood,
And the wild winds of passion shook my slim stem's
   maidenhood.

The trooping fawns at evening came and laid
   Their cool black noses on my lowest boughs,

And on my topmost branch the blackbird made
   A little nest of grasses for his spouse,
And now and then a twittering wren would light
On a thin twig which hardly bare the weight of such
   delight.

I was the Attic shepherd's trysting place,
   Beneath my shadow Amaryllis lay,   470
And round my trunk would laughing Daphnis chase
   The timorous girl, till tired out with play
She felt his hot breath stir her tangled hair,
And turned, and looked, and fled no more from such
   delightful snare.

Then come away unto my ambuscade
   Where clustering woodbine weaves a canopy
For amorous pleasaunce, and the rustling shade
   Of Paphian myrtles seems to sanctify
The dearest rites of love, there in the cool
And green recesses of its farthest depth there is a pool,   480

The ouzel's haunt, the wild bee's pasturage,
   For round its rim great creamy lilies float
Through their flat leaves in verdant anchorage,
   Each cup a white-sailed golden-laden boat
Steered by a dragon-fly, – be not afraid
To leave this wan and wave-kissed shore, surely the place
   was made

For lovers such as we, the Cyprian Queen,
   One arm around her boyish paramour,
Strays often there at eve, and I have seen
   The moon strip off her misty vestiture   490
For young Endymion's eyes, be not afraid,
The panther feet of Dian never tread that secret glade.

Nay if thou wil'st, back to the beating brine,
   Back to the boisterous billow let us go,

And walk all day beneath the hyaline
   Huge vault of Neptune's watery portico,
And watch the purple monsters of the deep
Sport in ungainly play, and from his lair keen Xiphias leap.

For if my mistress find me lying here
   She will not ruth or gentle pity show,   500
But lay her boar-spear down, and with austere
   Relentless fingers string the cornel bow,
And draw the feathered notch against her breast,
And loose the archèd cord, ay, even now upon the quest

I hear her hurrying feet, – awake, awake,
   Thou laggard in love's battle! once at least
Let me drink deep of passion's wine, and slake
   My parchèd being with the nectarous feast
Which even Gods affect! O come Love come,
Still we have time to reach the cavern of thine azure home.'   510

Scarce had she spoken when the shuddering trees
   Shook, and the leaves divided, and the air
Grew conscious of a God, and the grey seas
   Crawled backward, and a long and dismal blare
Blew from some tasselled horn, a sleuth-hound bayed,
And like a flame a barbèd reed flew whizzing down the
   glade.

And where the little flowers of her breast
   Just brake into their milky blossoming,
This murderous paramour, this unbidden guest,
   Pierced and struck deep in horrid chambering,   520
And ploughed a bloody furrow with its dart,
And dug a long red road, and cleft with wingèd death her
   heart.

Sobbing her life out with a bitter cry
   On the boy's body fell the Dryad maid,
Sobbing for incomplete virginity,
   And raptures unenjoyed, and pleasures dead,

And all the pain of things unsatisfied,
And the bright drops of crimson youth crept down her
    throbbing side.

Ah! pitiful it was to hear her moan,
    And very pitiful to see her die   530
Ere she had yielded up her sweets, or known
    The joy of passion, that dread mystery
Which not to know is not to live at all,
And yet to know is to be held in death's most deadly thrall.

But as it hapt the Queen of Cythere,
    Who with Adonis all night long had lain
Within some shepherd's hut in Arcady,
On team of silver doves and gilded wane
    Was journeying Paphos-ward, high up afar
From mortal ken between the mountains and the morning
    star,   540

And when low down she spied the hapless pair,
    And heard the Oread's faint despairing cry,
Whose cadence seemed to play upon the air
    As though it were a viol, hastily
She bade her pigeons fold each straining plume,
And dropt to earth and reached the strand, and saw their
    dolorous doom.

For as a gardener turning back his head
    To catch the last notes of the linnet, mows
With careless scythe too near some flower bed,
    And cuts the thorny pillar of the rose,   550
And with the flower's loosened loveliness
Strews the brown mould, or as some shepherd lad in
    wantonness

Driving his little flock along the mead
    Treads down two daffodils which side by side
Have lured the lady-bird with yellow brede
    And made the gaudy moth forget its pride,

Treads down their brimming golden chalices
Under light feet which were not made for such rude
   ravages,

Or as a schoolboy tired of his book
   Flings himself down upon the reedy grass   560
And plucks two water-lilies from the brook,
   And for a time forgets the hour glass,
Then wearies of their sweets, and goes his way,
And lets the hot sun kill them, even so these lovers lay.

And Venus cried, 'It is dread Artemis
   Whose bitter hand hath wrought this cruelty,
Or else that mightier maid whose care it is
   To guard her strong and stainless majesty
Upon the hill Athenian, – alas!
That they who loved so well unloved into Death's house
   should pass.   570

So with soft hands she laid the boy and girl
   In the great golden waggon tenderly,
Her white throat whiter than a moony pearl
   Just threaded with a blue vein's tapestry
Had not yet ceased to throb, and still her breast
Swayed like a wind-stirred lily in ambiguous unrest.

And then each pigeon spread its milky van,
   The bright car soared into the dawning sky,
And like a cloud the aerial caravan
   Passed over the Ægean silently,   580
Till the faint air was troubled with the song
From the wan mouths that call on bleeding Thammuz all
   night long.

But when the doves had reached their wonted goal
   Where the wide stair of orbèd marble dips
Its snows into the sea, her fluttering soul
   Just shook the trembling petals of her lips

And passed into the void, and Venus knew
That one fair maid the less would walk amid her retinue,

And bade her servants carve a cedar chest
   With all the wonder of this history,   590
Within whose scented womb their limbs should rest
   Where olive-trees make tender the blue sky
On the low hills of Paphos, and the faun
Pipes in the noonday, and the nightingale sings on till
   dawn.

Nor failed they to obey her hest, and ere
   The morning bee had stung the daffodil
With tiny fretful spear, or from its lair
   The waking stag had leapt across the rill
And roused the ouzel, or the lizard crept
Athwart the sunny rock, beneath the grass their bodies
   slept.   600

And when day brake, within that silver shrine
   Fed by the flames of cressets tremulous,
Queen Venus knelt and prayed to Proserpine
   That she whose beauty made Death amorous
Should beg a guerdon from her pallid Lord,
And let Desire pass across dread Charon's icy ford.

III

In melancholy moonless Acheron,
   Far from the goodly earth and joyous day,
Where no spring ever buds, nor ripening sun
   Weighs down the apple trees, nor flowery May   610
Chequers with chestnut blooms the grassy floor,
Where thrushes never sing, and piping linnets mate no
   more,

There by a dim and dark Lethæan well
   Young Charmides was lying, wearily
He plucked the blossoms from the asphodel,
   And with its little rifled treasury
Strewed the dull waters of the dusky stream,

And watched the white stars founder, and the land was like
   a dream,

When as he gazed into the watery glass
   And through his brown hair's curly tangles scanned   620
His own wan face, a shadow seemed to pass
   Across the mirror, and a little hand
Stole into his, and warm lips timidly
Brushed his pale cheeks, and breathed their secret forth into
   a sigh.

Then turned he round his weary eyes and saw,
   And ever nigher still their faces came,
And nigher ever did their young mouths draw
   Until they seemed one perefect rose of flame,
And longing arms around her neck he cast,
And felt her throbbing bosom, and his breath came hot and
   fast,   630

And all his hoarded sweets were hers to kiss,
   And all her maidenhood was his to slay,
And limb to limb in long and rapturous bliss
   Their passion waxed and waned, – O why essay
To pipe again of love too venturous reed!
Enough, enough that Erôs laughed upon that flowerless
   mead.

Too venturous poesy O why essay
   To pipe again of passion! fold thy wings
O'er daring Icarus and bid thy lay
   Sleep hidden in the lyre's silent strings,   640
Till thou hast found the old Castalian rill,
Or from the Lesbian waters plucked drowned Sappho's
   golden quill!

Enough, enough that he whose life had been
   A fiery pulse of sin, a splendid shame,
Could in the loveless land of Hades glean
   One scorching harvest from those fields of flame

Where passion walks with naked unshod feet
And is not wounded, – ah! enough that once their lips
   could meet

In that wild throb when all existences
   Seem narrowed to one single ecstasy   650
Which dies through its own sweetness and the stress
   Of too much pleasure, ere Persephone
Had bade them serve her by the ebon throne
Of the pale God who in the fields of Enna loosed her zone.

Athanasia

To that gaunt House of Art which lacks for naught
   Of all the great things men have saved from Time,
The withered body of a girl was brought
   Dead ere the world's glad youth had touched its prime,
And seen by lonely Arabs lying hid
In the dim womb of some black pyramid.

But when they had unloosed the linen band
   Which swathed the Egyptian's body, – lo! was found
Closed in the wasted hollow of her hand
   A little seed, which sown in English ground   10
Did wondrous snow of starry blossoms bear,
And spread rich odours through our springtide air.

With such strange arts this flower did allure
   That all forgotten was the asphodel,
And the brown bee, the lily's paramour,
   Forsook the cup where he was wont to dwell,
For not a thing of earth it seemed to be,
But stolen from some heavenly Arcady.

In vain the sad narcissus, wan and white
   At its own beauty, hung across the stream,   20

The purple dragon-fly had no delight
    With its gold dust to make his wings a-gleam,
Ah! no delight the jasmine-bloom to kiss,
Or brush the rain-pearls from the eucharis.

For love of it the passionate nightingale
    Forgot the hills of Thrace, the cruel king,
And the pale dove no longer cared to sail
    Through the wet woods at time of blossoming,
But round this flower of Egypt sought to float,
With silvered wing and amethystine throat. 30

While the hot sun blazed in his tower of blue
    A cooling wind crept from the land of snows,
And the warm south with tender tears of dew
    Drenched its white leaves when Hesperos uprose
Amid those sea-green meadows of the sky
On which the scarlet bars of sunset lie.

But when o'er wastes of lily-haunted field
    The tired birds had stayed their amorous tune,
And broad and glittering like an argent shield
    High in the sapphire heavens hung the moon, 40
Did no strange dream or evil memory make
Each tremulous petal of its blossoms shake?

Ah no! to this bright flower a thousand years
    Seemed but the lingering of a summer's day,
It never knew the tide of cankering fears
    Which turn a boy's gold hair to withered grey,
The dread desire of death it never knew,
Or how all folk that they were born must rue.

For we to death with pipe and dancing go,
    Nor would we pass the ivory gate again, 50
As some sad river wearied of its flow
    Through the dull plains, the haunts of common men,

Leaps lover-like into the terrible sea!
And counts it gain to die so gloriously.

We mar our lordly strength in barren strife
   With the world's legions led by clamorous care,
It never feels decay but gathers life
   From the pure sunlight and the supreme air,
We live beneath Time's wasting sovereignty,
It is the child of all eternity.   60

Impression du Matin

The Thames nocturne of blue and gold
   Changed to a Harmony in grey:
   A barge with ochre-coloured hay
Dropt from the wharf: and chill and cold

The yellow fog came creeping down
   The bridges, till the houses' walls
   Seemed changed to shadows, and S. Paul's
Loomed like a bubble o'er the town.

Then suddenly arose the clang
   Of waking life; the streets were stirred
   With country waggons: and a bird
Flew to the glistening roofs and sang.

But one pale woman all alone,
   The daylight kissing her wan hair,
   Loitered beneath the gas lamps' flare,
With lips of flame and heart of stone.

Impression: Le Reveillon

The sky is laced with fitful red,
The circling mists and shadows flee,
The dawn is rising from the sea,
Like a white lady from her bed.

And jagged brazen arrows fall
Athwart the feathers of the night,
And a long wave of yellow light
Breaks silently on tower and hall,

And spreading wide across the wold
Wakes into flight some fluttering bird,
And all the chestnut tops are stirred,
And all the branches streaked with gold.

Impressions

I

Les Silhouettes

The sea is flecked with bars of grey,
The dull dead wind is out of tune,
And like a withered leaf the moon
Is blown across the stormy bay.

Etched clear upon the pallid sand
Lies the black boat: a sailor boy
Clambers aboard in careless joy
With laughing face and gleaming hand.

And overhead the curlews cry,
Where through the dusky upland grass

The young brown-throated reapers pass,
Like silhouettes against the sky.

II

La Fuite de la Lune

To outer senses there is peace,
   A dreamy peace on either hand,
   Deep silence in the shadowy land,
Deep silence where the shadows cease.

   Save for a cry that echoes shrill
   From some lone bird disconsolate;
   A corn-crake calling to its mate;
The answer from the misty hill.

   And suddenly the moon withdraws
   Her sickle from the lightening skies,
   And to her sombre cavern flies,
Wrapped in a veil of yellow gauze.

In the Gold Room

A Harmony

Her ivory hands on the ivory keys
   Strayed in a fitful fantasy,
Like the silver gleam when the poplar trees
   Rustle their pale leaves listlessly,
   Or the drifting foam of a restless sea
When the waves show their teeth in the flying breeze.

Her gold hair fell on the wall of gold
   Like the delicate gossamer tangles spun
On the burnished disk of the marigold,
   Or the sun-flower turning to meet the sun

When the gloom of the dark blue night is done,
And the spear of the lily is aureoled.

And her sweet red lips on these lips of mine
 Burned like the ruby fire set
In the swinging lamp of a crimson shrine,
 Or the bleeding wounds of the pomegranate,
 Or the heart of the lotus drenched and wet
With the spilt-out blood of the rose-red wine.

Impressions

I

Le Jardin

The lily's withered chalice falls
 Around its rod of dusty gold,
 And from the beech trees on the wold
The last wood-pigeon coos and calls.

The gaudy leonine sunflower
 Hangs black and barren on its stalk,
 And down the wintry garden walk
The dead leaves scatter, – hour by hour.

Pale privet-petals white as milk
 Are blown into a snowy mass;
 The roses lie upon the grass,
Like little shreds of crimson silk.

II

La Mer

A white mist drifts across the shrouds,
 A wild moon in this wintery sky
 Gleams like an angry lion's eye
Out of a mane of tawny clouds.

The muffled steersman at the wheel
   Is but a shadow in the gloom;—
   And in the throbbing engine room
Leap the long rods of polished steel.

The shattered storm has left its trace
   Upon this huge and heaving dome,
   For the threads of yellow foam
Float on the waves like ravelled lace.

Le Jardin des Tuileries

This winter air is keen and cold,
   And keen and cold this winter sun,
   But round my chair the children run
Like little things of dancing gold.

Sometimes about the painted kiosk
   The mimic soldiers strut and stride,
   Sometimes the blue-eyed brigands hide
In the bleak tangles of the bosk.

And sometimes, while the old nurse cons
   Her book, they steal across the square,
   And launch their paper navies where
Huge Triton writhes in greenish bronze.

And now in mimic flight they flee,
   And now they rush, a boisterous band—
   And, tiny hand on tiny hand,
Climb up the black and leafless tree.

Ah! cruel tree! if I were you,
   And children climbed me, for their sake
   Though it be winter I would break
Into Spring blossoms white and blue!

The Harlot's House

We caught the tread of dancing feet,
We loitered down the moonlit street,
And stopped beneath the Harlot's house.

Inside, above the din and fray,
We heard the loud musicians play
The 'Treues Liebes Herz', of Strauss.

Like strange mechanical grotesques,
Making fantastic arabesques,
The shadows raced across the blind.

We watched the ghostly dancers spin   10
To sound of horn and violin,
Like black leaves wheeling in the wind.

Like wire-pulled automatons,
Slim silhouetted skeletons
Went sidling through the slow quadrille,

Then took each other by the hand,
And danced a stately saraband;
Their laughter echoed thin and shrill.

Sometimes a clock-work puppet pressed
A phantom lover to her breast,   20
Sometimes they seemed to try to sing,

Sometimes a horrible Marionette
Came out, and smoked its cigarette
Upon the steps like a live thing.

Then turning to my love I said,
'The dead are dancing with the dead,
The dust is whirling with the dust.'

But she, she heard the violin,
And left my side, and entered in;

Love passed into the house of Lust.   30

Then suddenly the tune went false,
The dancers wearied of the waltz,
The shadows ceased to wheel and whirl,

And down the long and silent street,
The dawn with silver-sandalled feet,
Crept like a frightened girl.

On the Sale by Auction of Keats' Love Letters

These are the letters which Endymion wrote
    To one he loved in secret, and apart.
    And now the brawlers of the auction mart
Bargain and bid for each poor blotted note,
Ay! for each separate pulse of passion quote
    The merchant's price: I think they love not art,
    Who break the crystal of a poet's heart
That small and sickly eyes may glare and gloat.

Is it not said that many years ago,
    In a far Eastern town, some soldiers ran
    With torches through the midnight, and began
To wrangle for mean raiment, and to throw
    Dice for the garments of a wretched man,
Not knowing the God's wonder, or His woe!

Fantasies Décoratives

I

Le Panneau

Under the rose-tree's dancing shade
   There stands a little ivory girl,
   Pulling the leaves of pink and pearl
With pale green nails of polished jade.

The red leaves fall upon the mould,
   The white leaves flutter, one by one,
   Down to a blue bowl where the sun,
Like a great dragon, writhes in gold.

The white leaves float upon the air,
   The red leaves flutter idly down,   10
   Some fall upon her yellow gown,
And some upon her raven hair.

She takes an amber lute and sings,
   And as she sings a silver crane
   Begins his scarlet neck to strain,
And flap his burnished metal wings.

She takes a lute of amber bright,
   And from the thicket where he lies
   Her lover, with his almond eyes,
Watches her movements in delight.   20

And now she gives a cry of fear,
   And tiny tears begin to start:
   A thorn has wounded with its dart
The pink-veined sea-shell of her ear.

And now she laughs a merry note:
   There has fallen a petal of the rose
   Just where the yellow satin shows
The blue-veined flower of her throat.

With pale green nails of polished jade,
   Pulling the leaves of pink and pearl,   30
   There stands a little ivory girl
Under the rose-tree's dancing shade.

II

Les Ballons

Against these turbid turquoise skies
   The light and luminous balloons
   Dip and drift like satin moons,
Drift like silken butterflies.

Reel with every windy gust,
   Rise and reel like dancing girls,
   Float like strange transparent pearls,
Fall and float like silver dust

Now to the low leaves they cling,
   Each with coy fantastic pose,
   Each a petal of a rose
Straining at a gossamer string.

Then to the tall trees they climb,
   Like thin globes of amethyst,
   Wandering opals keeping tryst
With the rubies of the lime.

Canzonet

I have no store
Of gryphon-guarded gold;
Now, as before,
Bare is the shepherd's fold.
Rubies, nor pearls,
Have I to gem thy throat;
Yet woodland girls
Have loved the shepherd's note.

Then, pluck a reed
And bid me sing to thee,
For I would feed
Thine ears with melody,
Who art more fair
Than fairest fleur-de-lys,
More sweet and rare
Than sweetest ambergris.

What dost thou fear?
Young Hyacinth is slain,
Pan is not here,
And will not come again.
No hornèd Faun
Treads down the yellow leas,
No God at dawn
Steals through the olive trees.

Hylas is dead,
Nor will he e'er divine
Those little red
Rose-petalled lips of thine.
On the high hill
No ivory Dryads play,
Silver and still
Sinks the sad autumn day.

Symphony in Yellow

An omnibus across the bridge
   Crawls like a yellow butterfly,
   And, here and there, a passer-by
Shows like a little restless midge.

Big barges full of yellow hay
   Are moored against the shadowy wharf,
   And, like a yellow silken scarf,
The thick fog hangs along the quay.

The yellow leaves begin to fade
   And flutter from the Temple elms,
   And at my feet the pale green Thames
Lies like a rod of rippled jade.

In the Forest

Out of the mid-woods' twilight
   Into the meadow's dawn,
Ivory-limbed and brown-eyed
   Flashes my Faun!

He skips through the copses singing,
   And his shadow dances along,
And I know not which I should follow,
   Shadow or song!

O Hunter, snare me his shadow!
   O Nightingale, catch me his strain!
Else moonstruck with music and madness
   I track him in vain.

La Circassienne

I love your tremulous topaz eyes
    That light with flame these midnight streets,
I love your body as it lies
    Like amber on the silken sheets.

I love the honey coloured hair
    That ripples to your ivory hips,
I love the tired listless air
    With which you kiss my boyish lips.

I love the wandering hyaline
    Blue vein that on your shoulder glows,
I love your pale pink nails which shine
    Like petals pilfered from the rose.

I love your mouth of vermilion,
    Your gilded breasts, your sun-scorched neck,
Which is as brown as cinnamon
    With here and there a purple fleck.

I love the bows that bend above
    Your eyelids of chalcedony,
And most of all, my love, I love,
    Your beautiful fierce chastity.

                                Cairo.

The Sphinx

In a dim corner of my room for longer than my fancy
    thinks
A beautiful and silent Sphinx has watched me through the
    shifting gloom.

Inviolate and immobile she does not rise she does not stir
For silver moons are naught to her and naught to her the
    suns that reel.

Red follows grey across the air the waves of moonlight ebb
    and flow
But with the dawn she does not go and in the night-time
    she is there.

Dawn follows dawn and nights grow old and all the while
    this curious cat
Lies couching on the Chinese mat with eyes of satin rimmed
    with gold.

Upon the mat she lies and leers and on the tawny throat of
    her
Flutters the soft and silky fur or ripples to her pointed ears.   10

Come forth my lovely seneschal! so somnolent, so
    statuesque!
Come forth you exquisite grotesque! half woman and half
    animal!

Come forth my lovely languorous Sphinx! and put your
    head upon my knee!
And let me stroke your throat and seek your body spotted
    like the lynx!

And let me touch those curving claws of yellow ivory and
    grasp
The tail that like a monstrous asp coils round your heavy
    velvet paws!

*

A thousand weary centuries are thine while I have hardly
    seen

Some twenty summers cast their green for autumn's gaudy
  liveries.

But you can read the hieroglyphs on the great sandstone
  obelisks,
And you have talked with Basilisks, and you have looked
  on Hippogriffs.   20

O tell me, were you standing by when Isis to Osiris knelt?
And did you watch the Egyptian melt her union for Antony

And drink the jewel-drunken wine and bend her head in
  mimic awe
To see the huge Proconsul draw the salted tunny from the
  brine?

And did you mark the Cyprian kiss white Adon on his
  catafalque?
And did you follow Amenalk, the god of Helipolis?

And did you talk with Thoth, and did you hear the moon-
  horned Io weep?
And know the painted kings who sleep beneath the wedge-
  shaped pyramid?

*

Lift up your large black satin eyes which are like cushions
  where one sinks!
Fawn at my feet fantastic Sphinx! and sing me all your
  memories!   30

Sing to me of the Jewish maid who wandered with the Holy
  Child,
And how you led them through the wild, and how they
  slept beneath your shade.

Sing to me of that odorous green eve when couching by the
  marge
You heard from Adrian's gilded barge the laughter of
  Antinous

And lapped the stream and fed your drouth and watched
  with hot and hungry stare

The ivory body of that rare young slave with his
    pomegranate mouth!

Sing to me of the labyrinth in which the twy-formed Bull
    was stalled!
Sing to me of the night you crawled across the temple's
    granite plinth

When through the purple corridors the screaming scarlet
    Ibis flew
In terror, and a horrid dew dripped from the moaning
    mandragores,   40

And the great torpid Crocodile within the tank shed slimy
    tears,
And tare the jewels from his ears and staggered back into
    the Nile,

And the priests cursed you with shrill psalms as in your
    claws you seized their Snake
And crept away with it to slake your passion by the
    shuddering palms!

                                         *

Who were your lovers? who were they who wrestled for
    you in the dust?
Which was the vessel of your lust? what leman had you,
    every day?

Did giant Lizards come and crouch before you on the reedy
    banks?
Did Gryphons with great metal flanks leap on you in your
    trampled couch?

Did monstrous Hippopotami come sidling toward you in the
    mist?
Did gilt-scaled Dragons writhe and twist with passion as
    you passed them by?   50

And from the brick-built Lycian Tomb what horrible
    Chimaera came
With fearful heads and fearful flame to breed new wonders
    from your womb?

*

Or had you shameful secret quests and did you harry to
    your home
Some nereid coiled in amber foam with curious rock crystal
    breasts?

Or did you treading through the froth call to the brown
    Sidonian
For tidings of Leviathan, Leviathan or Behemoth?

Or did you when the sun was set climb up the cactus-
    covered slope
To meet your swarthy Ethiop whose body was of polished
    jet?

Or did you while the earthen skiffs dropped down the grey
    Nilotic flats
At twilight and the flickering bats flew round the Temple's
    triple glyphs.   60

Steal to the border of the bar and swim across the silent
    lake
And slink into the vault and make the pyramid your
    Lúpanar

Till from each black sarcophagus rose up the painted
    swathèd dead?
Or did you lure unto your bed the ivory-horned
    Tragelaphos?

Or did you love the God of Flies who plagued the Hebrews
    and was splashed
With wine unto the waist? Or Pasht, who had green beryls
    for her eyes?

Or that young God, the Tyrian, who was more amorous
    than the dove
Of Ashtaroth? or did you love the God of the Assyrian

Whose wings, like strange transparent talc, rose high above
    his hawk-faced head,
Painted with silver and with red and ribbed with rods of
    oreichalch?   70

Or did huge Apis from his car leap down and lay before
    your feet
Big blossoms of the honey-sweet and honey-coloured
    nenuphar?

*

How subtle-secret is your smile! Did you love none then?
    Nay, I know
Great Ammon was your bedfellow! He lay with you beside
    the Nile!

The river-horses in the slime trumpeted when they saw him
    come
Odorous with Syrian galbanum and smeared with
    spikenard and with thyme.

He came along the river-bank like some tall galley argent-
    sailed,
He strode across the waters, mailed in beauty, and the
    waters sank.

He strode across the desert sand: he reached the valley
    where you lay:
He waited till the dawn of day: then touched your black
    breasts with his hand.

80

You kissed his mouth with mouths of flame: you made the
    hornèd god your own:
You stood behind him on his throne: you called him by his
    secret name.

You whispered monstrous oracles into the caverns of his
    ears:
With blood of goats and blood of steers you taught him
    monstrous miracles.

White Ammon was your bedfellow! Your chamber was the
    steaming Nile!
And with your curved archaic smile you watched his
    passion come and go.

*

With Syrian oils his brows were bright: and widespread as a
    tent at noon
His marble limbs made pale the moon and lent the day a
    larger light.

His long hair was nine cubits' span and coloured like that
    yellow gem
Which hidden in their garment's hem the merchants bring
    from Kurdistan.   90

His face was as the must that lies upon a vat of new-made
    wine:
The seas could not insapphirine the perfect azure of his
    eyes.

His thick soft throat was white as milk and threaded with
    thin veins of blue:
And curious pearls like frozen dew were broidered on his
    flowing silk.

                          *

On pearl and porphyry pedestalled he was too bright to look
    upon:
For on his ivory breast there shone the wondrous ocean-
    emerald,

That mystic moonlit jewel which some diver of the Colchian
    caves
Had found beneath the blackening waves and carried to the
    Colchian witch.

Before his gilded galiot ran naked vine-wreathed Corybants,
And lines of swaying elephants knelt down to draw his
    chariot,   100

And lines of swarthy Nubians bare up his litter as he rode
Down the great granite-paven road between the nodding
    peacock-fans.

The merchants brought him steatite from Sidon in their
    painted ships:

The meanest cup that touched his lips was fashioned from a
   chrysolite.

The merchants brought him cedar-chests of rich apparel
   bound with cords:
His train was borne by Memphian Lords: young Kings were
   glad to be his guests.

Ten hundred shaven priests did bow to Ammon's altar day
   and night,
Ten hundred lamps did wave their light through Ammon's
   carven house – and now

Foul snake and speckled adder with their young ones crawl
   from stone to stone
For ruined is the house and prone the great rose-marble
   monolith!   110

Wild ass or trotting jackal comes and couches in the
   mouldering gates:
Wild satyrs call unto their mates across the fallen fluted
   drums.

And on the summit of the pile the blue-faced ape of Horus
   sits
And gibbers while the figtree splits the pillars of the
   peristyle.

*

The god is scattered here and there: deep hidden in the
   windy sand
I saw his giant granite hand still clenched in impotent
   despair.

And many a wandering caravan of stately negroes silken-
   shawled,
Crossing the desert, halts appalled before the neck that
   none can span.

And many a bearded Bedouin draws back his yellow-striped
   burnous
To gaze upon the Titan thews of him who was thy paladin.   120

*

Go, seek his fragments on the moor and wash them in the
    evening dew,
And from their pieces make anew thy mutilated paramour!

Go, seek them where they lie alone and from their broken
    pieces make
Thy bruisèd bedfellow! and wake mad passions in the
    senseless stone!

Charm his dull ear with Syrian hymns! He loved your body!
    Oh, be kind,
Pour spikenard on his hair, and wind soft rolls of linen
    round his limbs!

Wind round his head the figured coins! Stain with red fruits
    those pallid lips!
Weave purple for his shrunken hips! and purple for his
    barren loins!

*

Away to Egypt! Have no fear. Only one God has ever died.
Only one God has let his side be wounded by a soldier's
    spear.   130

But these, thy lovers, are not dead. Still by the hundred-
    cubit gate
Dog-faced Anubis sits in state with lotus-lilies for thy head.

Still from his chair of porphyry gaunt Memnon strains his
    lidless eyes
Across the empty land, and cries each yellow morning unto
    thee.

And Nilus with his broken horn lies in his black and oozy
    bed
And till thy coming will not spread his waters on the
    withering corn.

Your lovers are not dead, I know. They will rise up and
    hear your voice
And clash their cymbals and rejoice and run to kiss your
    mouth! And so,

Set wings upon your argosies! Set horses to your ebon car!
Back to your Nile! Or if you are grown sick of dead divinities   140

Follow some roving lion's spoor across the copper-coloured
    plain,
Reach out and hale him by the mane and bid him be your
    paramour!

Couch by his side upon the grass and set your white teeth
    in his throat
And when you hear his dying note lash your long flanks of
    polished brass

And take a tiger for your mate, whose amber sides are
    flecked with black,
And ride upon his gilded back in triumph through the
    Theban gate,

And toy with him in amorous jests, and when he turns, and
    snarls, and gnaws,
O smite him with your jasper claws! and bruise him with
    your agate breasts!

                              *

Why are you tarrying? Get hence! I weary of your sullen
    ways,
I weary of your steadfast gaze, your somnolent
    magnificence.   150

Your horrible and heavy breath makes the light flicker in
    the lamp,
And on my brow I feel the damp and dreadful dews of night
    and death.

Your eyes are like fantastic moons that shiver in some
    stagnant lake,
Your tongue is like a scarlet snake that dances to fantastic
    tunes,

Your pulse makes poisonous melodies, and your black
    throat is like the hole
Left by some torch or burning coal on Saracenic tapestries.

Away! the sulphur-coloured stars are hurrying through the
    Western Gate!
Away! or it may be too late to climb their silent silver cars!

See, the dawn shivers round the grey gilt-dialled towers,
    and the rain
Streams down each diamonded pane and blurs with tears
    the wannish day.   160

What snake-tressed Fury fresh from Hell, with uncouth
    gestures and unclean,
Stole from the poppy-drowsy Queen and led you to a
    student's cell?

*

What songless tongueless Ghost of Sin crept through the
    curtains of the night,
And saw my taper burning bright, and knocked, and bade
    you enter in.

Are there not others more accursed, whiter with leprosies
    than I?
Are Abana and Pharphar dry that you come here to slake
    your thirst?

Get hence, you loathsome Mystery! Hideous animal, get
    hence!
You wake in me each bestial sense, you make me what I
    would not be.

You make my creed a barren sham, you wake foul dreams
    of sensual life,
And Atys with his blood-stained knife were better than the
    thing I am.   170

False Sphinx! False Sphinx! by reedy Styx old Charon,
    leaning on his oar,
Waits for my coin. Go thou before, and leave me to my
    Crucifix,

Whose pallid burden, sick with pain, watches the world
    with wearied eyes,

And weeps for every soul that dies, and weeps for every soul
    in vain.

In Memoriam
C. T. W.
Sometime Trooper of the Royal Horse Guards.
Obiit H.M. Prison, Reading, Berkshire,
July 7th, 1896.

The Ballad of Reading Gaol

By C.3.3.

I

He did not wear his scarlet coat,
    For blood and wine are red,
And blood and wine were on his hands
    When they found him with the dead,
The poor dead woman whom he loved,
    And murdered in her bed.

He walked amongst the Trial Men
    In a suit of shabby gray;
A cricket cap was on his head,
    And his step seemed light and gay;   10
But I never saw a man who looked
    So wistfully at the day.

I never saw a man who looked
    With such a wistful eye
Upon that little tent of blue
    Which prisoners call the sky,
And at every drifting cloud that went
    With sails of silver by.

I walked, with other souls in pain,
  Within another ring,   20
And was wondering if the man had done
  A great or little thing,
When a voice behind me whispered low,
  'That fellow's got to swing.'

Dear Christ! the very prison walls
  Suddenly seemed to reel,
And the sky above my head became
  Like a casque of scorching steel;
And, though I was a soul in pain,
  My pain I could not feel.   30

I only knew what hunted thought
  Quickened his step, and why
He looked upon the garish day
  With such a wistful eye;
The man had killed the thing he loved,
  And so he had to die.

*

Yet each man kills the thing he loves,
  By each let this be heard,
Some do it with a bitter look,
  Some with a flattering word,   40
The coward does it with a kiss,
  The brave man with a sword!

Some kill their love when they are young,
  And some when they are old;
Some strangle with the hands of Lust,
  Some with the hands of Gold:
The kindest use a knife, because
  The dead so soon grow cold.

Some love too little, some too long,
  Some sell, and others buy;   50
Some do the deed with many tears,
  And some without a sigh:

For each man kills the thing he loves,
    Yet each man does not die.

                                *

He does not die a death of shame
    On a day of dark disgrace,
Nor have a noose about his neck,
    Nor a cloth upon his face,
Nor drop feet foremost through the floor
    Into an empty space.   60

He does not sit with silent men
    Who watch him night and day;
Who watch him when he tries to weep,
    And when he tries to pray;
Who watch him lest himself should rob
    The prison of its prey.

He does not wake at dawn to see
    Dread figures throng his room,
The shivering Chaplain robed in white,
    The Sheriff stern with gloom,
And the Governor all in shiny black,   70
    With the yellow face of Doom.

He does not rise in piteous haste
    To put on convict-clothes,
While some coarse-mouthed Doctor gloats, and notes
    Each new and nerve-twitched pose,
Fingering a watch whose little ticks
    Are like horrible hammer-blows.

He does not know that sickening thirst
    That sands one's throat, before   80
The hangman with his gardener's gloves
    Slips through the padded door,
And binds one with three leathern thongs,
    That the throat may thirst no more.

He does not bend his head to hear
    The Burial Office read,

Nor, while the terror of his soul
   Tells him he is not dead,
Cross his own coffin, as he moves
   Into the hideous shed.   90

He does not stare upon the air
   Through a little roof of glass:
He does not pray with lips of clay
   For his agony to pass;
Nor feel upon his shuddering cheek
   The kiss of Caiaphas.

II

Six weeks our guardsman walked the yard,
   In the suit of shabby gray:
His cricket cap was on his head,
   And his step seemed light and gay,   100
But I never saw a man who looked
   So wistfully at the day.

I never saw a man who looked
   With such a wistful eye
Upon that little tent of blue
   Which prisoners call the sky,
And at every wandering cloud that trailed
   Its ravelled fleeces by.

He did not wring his hands, as do
   Those witless men who dare   110
To try to rear the changeling Hope
   In the cave of black Despair:
He only looked upon the sun,
   And drank the morning air.

He did not wring his hands nor weep,
   Nor did he peek or pine,
But he drank the air as though it held
   Some healthful anodyne;

With open mouth he drank the sun
   As though it had been wine!   120

And I and all the souls in pain,
   Who tramped the other ring,
Forgot if we ourselves had done
   A great or little thing,
And watched with gaze of dull amaze
   The man who had to swing.

And strange it was to see him pass
   With a step so light and gay,
And strange it was to see him look
   So wistfully at the day,   130
And strange it was to think that he
   Had such a debt to pay.

*

For oak and elm have pleasant leaves
   That in the spring-time shoot:
But grim to see is the gallows-tree,
   With its adder-bitten root,
And, green or dry, a man must die
   Before it bears its fruit!

The loftiest place is that seat of grace
   For which all wordlings try: 140
But who would stand in hempen band
   Upon a scaffold high,
And through a murderer's collar take
   His last look at the sky?

It is sweet to dance to violins
   When Love and Life are fair:
To dance to flutes, to dance to lutes
   Is delicate and rare:
But it is not sweet with nimble feet
   To dance upon the air!   150

So with curious eyes and sick surmise
   We watched him day by day,

And wondered if each one of us
   Would end the self-same way,
For none can tell to what red Hell
   His sightless soul may stray.

              *

At last the dead man walked no more
   Amongst the Trial Men,
And I knew that he was standing up
   In the black dock's dreadful pen,   160
And that never would I see his face
   In God's sweet world again.

Like two doomed ships that pass in storm
   We had crossed each other's way:
But we made no sign, we said no word,
   We had no word to say;
For we did not meet in the holy night,
   But in the shameful day.

A prison wall was round us both,
   Two outcast men we were: 170
The world had thrust us from its heart,
   And God from out His care:
And the iron gin that waits for Sin
   Had caught us in its snare.

III

In Debtors' Yard the stones are hard,
   And the dripping wall is high,
So it was there he took the air
   Beneath the leaden sky,
And by each side a Warder walked,
   For fear the man might die.   180

Or else he sat with those who watched
   His anguish night and day;

Who watched him when he rose to weep,
  And when he crouched to pray;
Who watched him lest himself should rob
  Their scaffold of its prey.

The Governor was strong upon
  The Regulations Act:
The Doctor said that Death was but
  A scientific fact: 190
And twice a day the Chaplain called,
  And left a little tract.

And twice a day he smoked his pipe,
  And drank his quart of beer:
His soul was resolute, and held
  No hiding-place for fear;
He often said that he was glad
  The hangman's hands were near.

But why he said so strange a thing
  No Warder dared to ask: 200
For he to whom a watcher's doom
  Is given as his task,
Must set a lock upon his lips,
  And make his face a mask.

Or else he might be moved, and try
  To comfort or console:
And what should Human Pity do
  Pent up in Murderers' Hole?
What word of grace in such a place
  Could help a brother's soul?   210

*

With slouch and swing around the ring
  We trod the Fools' Parade!
We did not care: we knew we were
  The Devil's Own Brigade:
And shaven head and feet of lead
  Make a merry masquerade.

We tore the tarry rope to shreds
  With blunt and bleeding nails;
We rubbed the doors, and scrubbed the floors,
  And cleaned the shining rails: 220
And, rank by rank, we soaped the plank,
  And clattered with the pails.

We sewed the sacks, we broke the stones,
  We turned the dusty drill:
We banged the tins, and bawled the hymns,
  And sweated on the mill:
But in the heart of every man
  Terror was lying still.

So still it lay that every day
  Crawled like a weed-clogged wave: 230
And we forgot the bitter lot
  That waits for fool and knave,
Till once, as we tramped in from work,
  We passed an open grave.

With yawning mouth the yellow hole
  Gaped for a living thing;
The very mud cried out for blood
  To the thirsty asphalte ring:
And we knew that ere one dawn grew fair
  Some prisoner had to swing.   240

Right in we went, with soul intent
  On Death and Dread and Doom:
The hangman, with his little bag,
  Went shuffling through the gloom:
And each man trembled as he crept
  Into his numbered tomb.

*

That night the empty corridors
  Were full of forms of Fear,
And up and down the iron town
  Stole feet we could not hear,   250

And through the bars that hide the stars
    White faces seemed to peer.

He lay as one who lies and dreams
    In a pleasant meadow-land,
The watchers watched him as he slept,
    And could not understand
How one could sleep so sweet a sleep
    With a hangman close at hand.

But there is no sleep when men must weep
    Who never yet have wept: 260
So we – the fool, the fraud, the knave—
    That endless vigil kept,
And through each brain on hands of pain
    Another's terror crept.

                    *

Alas! it is a fearful thing
    To feel another's guilt!
For, right within, the sword of Sin
    Pierced to its poisoned hilt,
And as molten lead were the tears we shed
    For the blood we had not spilt.   270

The Warders with their shoes of felt
    Crept by each padlocked door,
And peeped and saw, with eyes of awe,
    Gray figures on the floor,
And wondered why men knelt to pray
    Who never prayed before.

All through the night we knelt and prayed,
    Mad mourners of a corse!
The troubled plumes of midnight were
    The plumes upon a hearse: 280
And bitter wine upon a sponge
    Was the savour of Remorse.

                    *

The gray cock crew, the red cock crew,
    But never came the day:
And crooked shapes of Terror crouched,
    In the corners where we lay:
And each evil sprite that walks by night
    Before us seemed to play.

They glided past, they glided fast,
    Like travellers through a mist: 290
They mocked the moon in a rigadoon
    Of delicate turn and twist,
And with formal pace and loathsome grace
    The phantoms kept their tryst.

With mop and mow, we saw them go,
    Slim shadows hand in hand:
About, about, in ghostly rout
    They trod a saraband:
And the damned grotesques made arabesques,
    Like the wind upon the sand!   300

With pirouettes of marionettes,
    They tripped on pointed tread:
But with flutes of Fear they filled the ear,
    As their grisly masque they led,
And loud they sang, and long they sang,
    For they sang to wake the dead.

'Oho!' they cried, *'The world is wide,*
    But fettered limbs go lame!
And once, or twice, to throw the dice
    Is a gentlemanly game,   310
But he does not win who plays with Sin
    In the secret House of Shame.'

*

No things of air these antics were,
    That frolicked with such glee:
To men whose lives were held in gyves,
    And whose feet might not go free,

Ah! wounds of Christ! they were living things,
   Most terrible to see.

Around, around, they waltzed and wound;
   Some wheeled in smirking pairs;   320
With the mincing step of a demirep
   Some sidled up the stairs:
And with subtle sneer, and fawning leer,
   Each helped us at our prayers.

                    *

The morning wind began to moan,
   But still the night went on:
Through its giant loom the web of gloom
   Crept till each thread was spun:
And, as we prayed, we grew afraid
   Of the Justice of the Sun.   330

The moaning wind went wandering round
   The weeping prison-wall:
Till like a wheel of turning steel
   We felt the minutes crawl:
O moaning wind! what had we done
   To have such a seneschal?

At last I saw the shadowed bars,
   Like a lattice wrought in lead,
Move right across the whitewashed wall
   That faced my three-plank bed,   340
And I knew that somewhere in the world
   God's dreadful dawn was red.

                    *

At six o'clock we cleaned our cells,
   At seven all was still,
But the sough and swing of a mighty wing
   The prison seemed to fill,
For the Lord of Death with icy breath
   Had entered in to kill.

He did not pass in purple pomp,
    Nor ride a moon-white steed.   350
Three yards of cord and a standing board
    Are all the gallows' need:
So with rope of shame the Herald came
    To do the secret deed.

*

We were as men who through a fen
    Of filthy darkness grope:
We did not dare to breathe a prayer,
    Or to give our anguish scope:
Something was dead in each of us,
    And what was dead was Hope.   360

For Man's grim Justice goes its way,
    And will not swerve aside:
It slays the weak, it slays the strong,
    It has a deadly stride:
With iron heel it slays the strong,
    The monstrous parricide!

*

We waited for the stroke of eight:
    Each tongue was thick with thirst:
For the stroke of eight is the stroke of Fate
    That makes a man accursed,   370
And Fate will use a running noose
    For the best man and the worst.

We had no other thing to do,
    Save to wait for the sign to come:
So, like things of stone in a valley lone,
    Quiet we sat and dumb:
But each man's heart beat thick and quick,
    Like a madman on a drum!

*

With sudden shock the prison-clock
    Smote on the shivering air,   380

And from all the gaol rose up a wail
    Of impotent despair,
Like the sound that frightened marshes hear
    From some leper in his lair.

And as one sees most fearful things
    In the crystal of a dream,
We saw the greasy hempen rope
    Hooked to the blackened beam,
And heard the prayer the hangman's snare
    Strangled into a scream.   390

And all the woe that moved him so
    That he gave that bitter cry,
And the wild regrets, and bloody sweats,
    None knew so well as I:
For he who lives more lives than one
    More deaths than one must die.

                        IV

There is no chapel on the day
    On which they hang a man:
The Chaplain's heart is far too sick,
    Or his face is far too wan,   400
Or there is that written in his eyes
    Which none should look upon.

So they kept us close till nigh on noon,
    And then they rang the bell,
And the Warders with their jingling keys
    Opened each listening cell,
And down the iron stair we tramped,
    Each from his separate Hell.

Out into God's sweet air we went,
    But not in wonted way,   410
For this man's face was white with fear,
    And that man's face was gray,

And I never saw sad men who looked
    So wistfully at the day.

I never saw sad men who looked
    With such a wistful eye
Upon the little tent of blue
    We prisoners called the sky,
And at every careless cloud that passed
    In happy freedom by.   420

But there were those amongst us all
    Who walked with downcast head,
And knew that, had each got his due,
    They should have died instead:
He had but killed a thing that lived,
    Whilst they had killed the dead.

For he who sins a second time
    Wakes a dead soul to pain,
And draws it from its spotted shroud,
    And makes it bleed again,   430
And makes it bleed great gouts of blood,
    And makes it bleed in vain!

                          *

Like ape or clown, in monstrous garb
    With crooked arrows starred,
Silently we went round and round
    The slippery asphalte yard;
Silently we went round and round,
    And no man spoke a word.

Silently we went round and round,
    And through each hollow mind   440
The Memory of dreadful things
    Rushed like a dreadful wind,
And Horror stalked before each man,
    And Terror crept behind.

                          *

The Warders strutted up and down,
  And kept their herd of brutes,
Their uniforms were spick and span,
  And they wore their Sunday suits,
But we knew the work they had been at,
  By the quicklime on their boots.   450

For where a grave had opened wide,
  There was no grave at all:
Only a stretch of mud and sand
  By the hideous prison-wall,
And a little heap of burning lime,
  That the man should have his pall.

For he has a pall, this wretched man,
  Such as few can claim:
Deep down below a prison-yard,
  Naked for greater shame,   460
He lies, with fetters on each foot,
  Wrapt in a sheet of flame!

And all the while the burning lime
  Eats flesh and bone away,
It eats the brittle bone by night,
  And the soft flesh by day,
It eats the flesh and bone by turns,
  But it eats the heart alway.

*

For three long years they will not sow
  Or root or seedling there: 470
For three long years the unblessed spot
  Will sterile be and bare,
And look upon the wondering sky
  With unreproachful stare.

They think a murderer's heart would taint
  Each simple seed they sow.
It is not true! God's kindly earth
  Is kindlier than men know,

And the red rose would but blow more red,
   The white rose whiter blow.   480

Out of his mouth a red, red rose!
   Out of his heart a white!
For who can say by what strange way,
   Christ brings His will to light,
Since the barren staff the pilgrim bore
   Bloomed in the great Pope's sight?

*

But neither milk-white rose nor red
   May bloom in prison air;
The shard, the pebble, and the flint,
   Are what they give us there: 490
For flowers have been known to heal
   A common man's despair.

So never will wine-red rose or white,
   Petal by petal, fall
On that stretch of mud and sand that lies
   By the hideous prison-wall,
To tell the men who tramp the yard
   That God's Son died for all.

*

Yet though the hideous prison-wall
   Still hems him round and round,   500
And a spirit may not walk by night
   That is with fetters bound,
And a spirit may but weep that lies
   In such unholy ground,

He is at peace – this wretched man—
   At peace, or will be soon:
There is no thing to make him mad,
   Nor does Terror walk at noon,
For the lampless Earth in which he lies
   Has neither Sun nor Moon.   510

*

They hanged him as a beast is hanged:
    They did not even toll
A requiem that might have brought
    Rest to his startled soul,
But hurriedly they took him out,
    And hid him in a hole.

They stripped him of his canvas clothes,
    And gave him to the flies:
They mocked the swollen purple throat,
    And the stark and staring eyes: 520
And with laughter loud they heaped the shroud
    In which their convict lies.

The Chaplain would not kneel to pray
    By his dishonoured grave:
Nor mark it with that blessed Cross
    That Christ for sinners gave,
Because the man was one of those
    Whom Christ came down to save.

Yet all is well; he has but passed
    To Life's appointed bourne: 530
And alien tears will fill for him
    Pity's long-broken urn,
For his mourners will be outcast men,
    And outcasts always mourn.

V

I know not whether Laws be right,
    Or whether Laws be wrong;
All that we know who lie in gaol
    Is that the wall is strong;
And that each day is like a year,
    A year whose days are long.   540

But this I know, that every Law
    That men have made for Man,

Since first Man took his brother's life,
    And the sad world began,
But straws the wheat and saves the chaff
    With a most evil fan.

This too I know – and wise it were
    If each could know the same—
That every prison that men build
    Is built with bricks of shame,   550
And bound with bars lest Christ should see
    How men their brothers maim.

With bars they blur the gracious moon,
    And blind the goodly sun:
And they do well to hide their Hell,
    For in it things are done
That Son of God nor son of Man
    Ever should look upon!

*

The vilest deeds like poison weeds
    Bloom well in prison-air: 560
It is only what is good in Man
    That wastes and withers there:
Pale Anguish keeps the heavy gate,
    And the Warder is Despair.

For they starve the little frightened child
    Till it weeps both night and day:
And they scourge the weak, and flog the fool,
    And gibe the old and gray,
And some grow mad, and all grow bad,
    And none a word may say.   570

Each narrow cell in which we dwell
    Is a foul and dark latrine,
And fetid breath of living Death
    Chokes up each grated screen,
And all, but Lust, is turned to dust
    In Humanity's machine.

The brackish water that we drink
  Creeps with a loathsome slime,
And the bitter bread they weigh in scales
  Is full of chalk and lime,   580
And Sleep will not lie down, but walks
  Wild-eyed, and cries to Time.

                    *

But though lean Hunger and green Thirst
  Like asp with adder fight,
We have little care of prison fare,
  For what chills and kills outright
Is that every stone one lifts`by day
  Becomes one's heart by night.

With midnight always in one's heart,
  And twilight in one's cell,   590
We turn the crank, or tear the rope,
  Each in his separate Hell,
And the silence is more awful far
  Than the sound of a brazen bell.

And never a human voice comes near
  To speak a gentle word:
And the eye that watches through the door
  Is pitiless and hard:
And by all forgot, we rot and rot,
  With soul and body marred.   600

And thus we rust Life's iron chain
  Degraded and alone:
And some men curse, and some men weep,
  And some men make no moan:
But God's eternal Laws are kind
  And break the heart of stone.

                    *

And every human heart that breaks,
  In prison-cell or yard,
Is as that broken box that gave

Its treasure to the Lord,   610
And filled the unclean leper's house
    With the scent of costliest nard.

Ah! happy they whose hearts can break
    And peace of pardon win!
How else may man make straight his plan
    And cleanse his soul from Sin?
How else but through a broken heart
    May Lord Christ enter in?

                    *

And he of the swollen purple throat,
    And the stark and staring eyes,   620
Waits for the holy hands that took
    The Thief to Paradise;
And a broken and a contrite heart
    The Lord will not despise.

The man in red who reads the Law
    Gave him three weeks of life,
Three little weeks in which to heal
    His soul of his soul's strife,
And cleanse from every blot of blood
    The hand that held the knife.   630

And with tears of blood he cleansed the hand,
    The hand that held the steel:
For only blood can wipe out blood,
    And only tears can heal:
And the crimson stain that was of Cain
    Became Christ's snow-white seal.

                   VI

In Reading gaol by Reading town
    There is a pit of shame,
And in it lies a wretched man
    Eaten by teeth of flame,   640

In a burning winding-sheet he lies,
 And his grave has got no name.

And there, till Christ call forth the dead,
 In silence let him lie:
No need to waste the foolish tear,
 Or heave the windy sigh:
The man had killed the thing he loved,
 And so he had to die.

And all men kill the thing they love,
 By all let this be heard,   650
Some do it with a bitter look,
 Some with a flattering word,
The coward does it with a kiss,
 The brave man with a sword!

        C.3.3

Notes

p. 3 Hélas!: the title means 'alas', and it is described by Wilde as the 'proem' or preface to the *Poems* of 1881. It sets the tone of poeticised regret which characterises so much of his verse.

p. 3 Sonnet to Liberty: published in 1881, it appeared with 'Theoretikos' in the first section of the volume, entitled 'Eleutheria', meaning 'freedom'. These poems have 'public' or political themes, and provide a contrast to the more sensuous and 'Aesthetic' tendencies with which Wilde's verse is associated.

p. 4 Theoretikos: published in the 1881 volume, the title means 'The Contemplative', and advocates a rejection of action in the interest of 'Art/ And loftiest culture'. This stance is more characteristic of Wilde, whose later writings would expound the 'Importance of Doing Nothing' (subtitle of 'The Critic as Artist', 1890). **l.5 that voice**: William Wordsworth (born 1770), English Romantic poet, and Laureate from 1843 to his death in 1850.

p. 4 Requiescat: published in the 1881 edition and revised in 1882, the title means 'May she rest'. It was probably written for Wilde's sister Isola who died in 1867 aged eight.

p. 5 San Miniato: first published in *The Dublin University Magazine*, in 1876, as the first part of 'Graffiti D'Italia. San Miniato. (June 15)'. Parts two and three of this were subsequently published as 'By the Arno' when they appeared with 'San Miniato' in 1881 (see introduction to the present volume). Wilde visited San Miniato, which is near Florence, in 1875. **l.3 Angel-Painter**: Fra Angelico (c. 1400–55), Italian painter and Dominican Friar who is famous for his frescoes at San Marco, his own friary and the subject of Wilde's poem.

p. 6 Sonnet: On Hearing the Dies Iræ Sung in the Sistine chapel: first published in *Lyra Hibernica Sacra*, ed. William MacIlwane (1878), and revised for the 1881 volume. **Dies Iræ**: means day of wrath and refers to the Last Judgment. The hymn is used in the Roman Catholic Mass for the dead.

p. 6 *Ave Maria Plena Gratia*: first published in the *Irish Monthly*, July 1878, as 'Ave Maria Gratia Plena' – hail Mary full of grace – the more correct form for this Catholic address. (The original title was restored in the *Collected Works*, edited by Robert Ross and published in 1908.) The sonnet evokes painterly treatments of the Annunciation of the Virgin. However, notwithstanding the Italian postscripts for the poem (Rome for the 1878 version, Florence for the 1881), the painting to which Wilde's 'description' most closely corresponds perhaps is Dante Gabriel Rossetti's *Ecce Ancilla Domini* (1850), an Annunciation painting which includes all the details to which the poem alludes. **l.4 Danae**: in Greek mythology, she was confined to a brazen tower, but Zeus descended upon her in the form of a shower of gold. **l.5 Semele**: visited by Zeus in 'the splendour of a God', and consumed by his lightning.

p. 7 *Madonna Mia*: first published in a different form as 'Wasted Days (From a Painting by Miss V. T.)', in *Kottabos*, vol. 3, 1877. The title means simply 'my lady', and, like 'Ave Maria' and 'La Bella Donna Della Mia Mente', is written in the Rossettian mode, combining sensuous celebrations of female beauty with mystical and literary allusions. Furthermore, like many of Rossetti's own sonnets, it is written for a painting. It also makes reference to the *Divine Comedy* of Dante Aligheri (1265–1321), a work which contributed to Rossetti's own personal symbolism for both his paintings and poems. In an early statement Wilde referred to himself as a 'Pre-Raphaelite', claiming artistic kinship with Rossetti as well as Burne-Jones and Morris (Mason, p. 326). For Wilde's adulation of these artists see 'The Garden of Eros', lines 157–207.

p. 7 *Untitled (O Golden Queen of life and joy)*: an unpublished poem taken from a transcription made by Walter Ledger in 1908 of the manuscript held by Ross (see Note on the Text). It apostrophes Helen of Troy, and was probably written for Lillie Langtry, the famous beauty, socialite and actress whom Wilde met in 1877. **l.9 poppy**: used for opiates, but also associated with death and forgetfulness (Morpheus, from which the word morphine derives, was the god of sleep and dreams). **l.10 mandragore**: a narcotic, believed to have aphrodisiac properties. **l.11 purple fruit**: probably the lotus, used by both Homer (*Odyssey*, bk. 9) and Tennyson ('The Lotos-Eaters') as a symbol for luxuriant dalliance and forgetfulness. l.16 **nepenthe**: a narcotic drink.

p. 8 Tristitiæ: first published in *Dublin University Magazine*, vol. 88, 1876, as 'Αἴλιον, αἴλινον, εἰπέ, τὸ, δ' εὖ νικάτω' – which means 'Sing a strain of woe, but let the good prevail!' – it subsequently appeared without a title in MacIlwane's *Lyra Hibernica Sacra* (1878), from which this version is taken. The title 'Tristitiæ' appeared on the original manuscript version of the poem, and in collections after 1913. It is retained here to aid identification. **l. 12 Builds ladders to be nearer God**: see Genesis, 28:12.

p. 9 Desespoir: despair. First published after Wilde's death when the manuscript was 'discovered' by Robert Ross, Wilde's executor, some time in 1908, and included in the second edition of the collected *Poems* (1909). The text for this poem is taken from a transcription made by Walter Ledger in November 1908 (see Note on the Text). Whilst Ross printed 'The seasons *send* their ruin', the transcript made by Ledger gives 'mend'; this has been followed because it is appropriate to the emphasis on cyclic renewal in the first lines of the poem.

p. 9 The Grave of Keats: this sonnet first appeared in an article entitled 'The Tomb of Keats', in the *Irish Monthly*, July 1877. It was revised for publication in the *Burlington Magazine*, vol. 1, January 1881, and revised further for the 1881 volume. The version used is from a facsimile of Wilde's manuscript for the 1881 *Poems*, which was reproduced in the Anderson Galleries Catalogue of the Sale of John B. Stetson, 23 April, 1920, p. 43. John Keats (born 1795) was a Romantic poet whose verse was largely unappreciated during his short life, but was enormously influential for many Victorian poets, including Rossetti, Tennyson, Swinburne and Wilde himself. He died in Rome in February 1821 of tuberculosis. His gravestone reads: 'Here lies one whose name was writ in water'. **l. 5 Sebastian**: a Christian saint who was martyred in 288. Wilde's theme of the Romantic poet as martyr, both in this sonnet and in the article of which it originally formed a part, would play an important role in his life and art. He would return to it in his sonnet 'On the Sale by Auction of Keats' Love Letters', and most fully in the writings following his trial and incarceration, *De Profundis*, and *The Ballad of Reading Gaol*. Wilde would take the christian name Sebastian when he was released from prison in 1897. **l. 10 Mitylene**: a town in Lesbos, the home of the poet Sappho. **l. 14 Isabella . . . Basil-Tree**: refers to a poem published by Keats in 1820, 'Isabella, or The Pot of Basil', which tells how Isabella kept the head of her lover, whom her brothers had trecherously slain, in a pot of basil: 'And so she ever fed it with thin tears'.

p. 10 Magdalen Walks: first published in a longer form in the *Irish Monthly*, vol. 6, April 1878, and revised for 1881 when three stanzas were omitted. The revision of this poem is significant, and reflects the change in Wilde's aesthetic taking place at this time. The omitted stanzas had introduced the 'I' of the poet, who broods on the brevity of life, into the landscape. By omitting these stanzas he purges the poem of its Wordsworthian elements, thus shifting its register from the Romantic to the more descriptive mode which he was increasingly adopting for his verse. **Magdalen**: (pronounced 'maudelen') the Oxford college where Wilde was an undergraduate from 1874 to 1878. Its grounds include a number of riverside walks.

p. 11 Chanson: the title means 'song', and was originally the second part of a poem entitled 'ΔΗΕΙΘΥΜΟΝ ΕΡΩΤΟΣ ΑΝΘΟΣ' ('The Rose of Love and with a rose's thorns'), appearing in *Kottabos*, vol. 2, 1876. The first part would later become 'La Bella Donna Della Mia Mente', when both parts were revised for the 1881 volume. Taken together, these ballads, with their combination of the fleshly, the mystical and the 'courtly' are reminiscent of many of Rossetti's poems. The comparison between the lady's hair and ripened corn in line 16 of 'La Bella Donna' recalls Rossetti's use of a similar image in 'The Blessed Damozel', whose hair 'Was yellow like ripe corn'. The Greek title is taken from the *Agamemnon* of Aeschylus, and refers once more to Helen of Troy.

p. 11 Pan: Double Villanelle: first published with 'Desespoir' by Robert Ross in the 1909 collected *Poems*. The text for this poem is taken from a copy made by Walter Ledger in November 1908 of the manuscript used by Ross for this edition. The text used here differs from the text found in Ross's edition only in minor details. Ross would often correct Wilde's punctuation and grammar. Thus in line 36 of 'Pan' Wilde had written 'give *thy* oaten pipes away', which Ross corrected to the more grammatical 'thine'. This ammendation has been adopted here. In line 26 Ross printed the initial letter in 'Liberty' in lower case, whereas Wilde capitalized it. A shorter version of this poem had appeared in the first issue of *Pan* in September 1880. Pan was a popular figure in turn-of-the-century literary culture, depicted by writers as diverse as Arthur Machen (*The Great God Pan*, 1895) and Kenneth Grahame (*The Wind in the Willows*, 1908). **l. 13 Helicé**: legendary princess of Arcadia.

p. 13 **from *The Garden of Eros*:** this poem appeared for the first time in the 1881 edition, and was revised in 1882. With its evocation of a 'Classicised' Oxford landscape, it recalls Matthew Arnold's 'Thyrsis' and 'The Scholar Gipsy', which combine imagery from the Classical pastoral tradition with references to the Oxfordshire countryside. The former is also an elegy, lamenting the loss of a poet (Arnold's friend Arthur Hugh Clough, 1819–61), and therefore corresponds to the partly elegiac aspect of Wilde's poem. 'Eros' is also a pantheon, which eulogises poets and artists (both Romantic and Victorian) as votaries of what Wilde terms the 'Spirit of Beauty' (see the introduction to the present volume). **l. 20 Dis:** the Roman term for the Underworld and its ruler. **l. 121 the boy who loved thee best:** refers to John Keats, the poet whom Percy Bysshe Shelley – 'One silver voice' – (1792–1822) had addressed as the eponymous figure in his pastoral elegy *Adonais* (1821). **l. 133 that fiery heart:** refers to Algernon Charles Swinburne (1837–1909), a poet infamous for his inflammatory politics and 'immoral' verses, to whom Wilde sent a copy of his *Poems* in 1881. **l. 146 Galilæan's requiem:** refers to Swinburne's 'Hymn to Proserpine' (1866), which celebrated paganism to the disparagement of Christianity; **l. 150 the new Sign:** therefore refers to the cross. **l. 157 Morris ... Chaucer's child:** William Morris (1834–96), craftsman, socialist and poet who was associated with the Pre-Raphaelite movement and an advocate for a picturesque Medievalism. **l. 158 Spenser:** the reference to Edmund Spenser (poet *c.* 1552–99) alludes to Morris's long verse Romances, dealing with Classical and Medieval themes, developing a genre perfected by Spenser in his *The Faerie Queene* (1596). **l. 161 flowerless fields of ice:** refers to Morris's interest in Icelandic sagas, some of which he translated in 1876 as *Sigurd the Volsung*; **ll. 163–7 Gudrun ... Aslaug ... Olafson ...:** characters from 'The Earthly Paradise' (1868–70) a poem by Morris. **l. 175 eight:** a rowing crew. **l. 176 Bagley:** woods near Oxford referred to by Arnold in 'The Scholar Gipsy' (1851), **l. 200 Dante ... Gabriel:** refers to Dante Gabriel Rossetti, poet and painter, one of the founders of the Pre-Raphaelite Brotherhood in 1848 (see notes for 'Ave Maria' and 'Madonna Mia'). **l. 203 Merlin ... Vivien:** refers to *The Beguiling of Merlin* (1874), a painting by Edward Burne-Jones (1833–98), friend of Rossetti and Morris and of Wilde, who followed and even surpassed his master Rossetti in the depiction of escapist mythological subjects, and studies in languid and ornate female beauty, such as 'The Golden Stairs' (1880). **l. 226 chastest mystery:** refers to the tradition in Classical myth that the moon (associated with the goddess Diana or Cynthia) was a virgin; by literalising this poetic trope (the myth of Actaeon who spied on Diana), Wilde gives this

Romantic lament a somewhat humorous cast. **l. 227 the last Endymion**: by adopting this persona the speaker once more invokes Keats, whom Wilde, in a poem 'On the Sale by Auction of Keats' Love Letters', fashioned as 'Endymion', after Keats's poem of that name which tells how Endymion falls in love with the moon (1818). Wilde's allusion to Keats in this stanza is appropriate given its theme of how science (represented by the telescope) desecrates beauty. Keats had similarly inveighed against this perceived process, complaining how Newton's *Optics* had destroyed all the poetry of the rainbow by reducing it to 'prismatic colours'. **l. 242 Natural Warfare**: alludes to what has been termed 'Social Darwinism', the use of a version of Evolutionary biology to justify ruthless social and economic practices.

p. 19 La Bella Donna Della Mia Mente: ('The Beautiful Lady of my Memory'). See notes for 'Chanson' above. **1.21 melilote**: a form of clover, renowned for its sweetness.

p. 20 By the Arno: originally part of 'Graffiti D'Italia. San Miniato (June 15)'. See notes for 'San Miniato', and the introduction to the present volume. **l. 8 Attic**: Athenian.

p. 21 Charmides: published in 1881 and revised for 1882, it is Wilde's longest poem. An 'Ovidian' erotic narrative, it is written in the tradition of Shakespeare's *Venus and Adonis* and Marlowe's *Hero and Leander* (both 1593). It was an ambitious project for a young poet to attempt. However, Wilde is not unsuccessful in handling its ingenious and sensuous passages of 'word-painting'. On the whole he manages to sustain the narrative momentum, and its erudition and Classical allusion are more appropriate and effectively conveyed in this poem than in others from this period. The theme of a young man's desire for a work of art has a number of sources, including the myth of Pygmalion (handled by Burne-Jones in 1868–70), and was an appropriate one for Wilde who was increasingly promoting himself as an 'Aesthete', and apostle of art. It is when Charmides attempts to embrace the 'real' Athena rather than her sculpted image that he is drowned. However, there is another possible explanation for Wilde's use of the temple violation scene. It can perhaps be understood in terms of 'Victorian' as much as Classical motivations or sources – a parallel with practices adopted by Victorian painters can be suggested. It has been remarked how many painters at the time circumvented 'official' morality by depicting nudes in Classical scenes, often giving their skin the quality of marble and thus the appearance of statues. These devices, adopted when such respectable Academicians as Lawrence Alma-Tadema (1836–1912) and Edward Poynter (1836–1919) depicted Classical nudes, served to displace the potential 'fleshliness' of their portrayals. Wilde is perhaps adopting a version of this stratagem in his representation of the erotic encounter between the youth and the statue. He can thus veil his references to the 'secret mystery' of Athena's 'pale and argent body undisplayed', with an aestheticised chasteness, and escape the kind of censure which was levied at Rossetti and Swinburne's 'fleshly' depictions of erotic love in the early 1870s. Significantly, when the poet comes to describe the encounter between Charmides and the Dryad in the final stanzas, he affects coyness and declines to attempt the task. **l. 27 fane**: a temple, in this case the temple to Athena, the patroness of Athens, which stood on the summit of the Acropolis in that city. The temple, called the 'Parthenon' (*c.* 432 B.C.), housed the statue of Athena Nike (Victory), by Phidias – an image which appears to correspond to the details of the statue adored by Charmides. This particular statue was, however, colossal, making Charmides' erotic profanation of it somewhat ludicrous if not impossible. **ll. 65–72 Griffin ... Gorgon's head ... owl**: refer to decorative details on the statue, the owl being the symbol for Athena. **l. 86 twelve Gods**: refers to the frieze depicting the Gods of Olympus which surrounded the Parthenon, parts of which now reside in London's British Museum. **ll. 93–4 terrible maidenhood ... pitiless chastity**: refer to the tradition that Athena was a virgin and that the *Parthenon* means temple of the maiden. **l.95 wight**: an archaic term for person. **l. 96 Troy's young shepherd**: Paris, who was given the opportunity to judge the charms of three goddesses. **l. 172 Bassarid**: a votary of Dionysus. **l. 216 Pallas**: a term often used to refer to Athena. **l. 286 diapered**: variegated or striped. **l. 301 Dryads**: wood-nymphs, trees which contain the spirits of young girls. **l. 334 lilies white and red**: poetic shorthand in the courtly tradition for attributes of (usually female) beauty. **l. 358 froward**: obstinate or naughty. **l. 360 three days since ... Proserpine**: a poetic way of saying that Charmides died three days ago, Proserpine being the queen of the Underworld. **l. 414 Hermes**: the winged messenger of the gods, called Mercury by the Romans. **l. 431 oath to Artemis**: that the Dryad, like the goddess, would remain chaste. **ll. 436–7 spouse for Cytheræa**: suitable for love. **l. 487 Cyprian Queen**: refers to Aphrodite who hailed from Cyprus. **l. 488 boyish paramour**: refers to Adonis, in one tradition the beloved of Aphrodite. **l. 499 my mistress**: Artemis. **l. 535 Cythere**: also denotes Aphrodite. **l. 542 Oread**: nymph. **l. 545 pigeons**: the doves which traditionally accompany the goddess of love. **l. 567 mightier maid**: the phrase refers to Aphrodite, but appeared as 'mightier may' in both the 1881 and 1882 editions. According to Stuart Mason, the misprint was recognised by Wilde and corrected by hand in copies which he presented to friends (Mason, p. 305). **l. 582 Thammuz**: the Syrian equivalent of Adonis. **l. 605 guerdon**: reward. **l. 606 Charon's icy ford**: the river Styx, over which Charon ferrys the dead. **l. 607 Acheron**: a river in the Underworld. **l. 641 Castalian rill**: a spring at the foot of mount Parnassus, sacred to Apollo and the Muses and therefore to poetry. **l. 642 Lesbian waters . . . Sappho's golden quill**: the island of Lesbos was the birth place of Sappho (7th C. B.C.), the lyric poet who reputedly drowned herself. **l. 645 Hades**: king of the Underworld, also the name given to his realm.

p. 42 *Athanasia*: originally published in *Time*, April 1879, as 'The Conqueror of Time', it was revised for 1881, and given the present title which means immortality. **l. 34 Hesperos**: the evening star.

p. 44 *Impression du Matin*: 'impression of the morning'; first published in *The World*, March 2 1881, it was revised for the 1881 volume. This poem marks Wilde's transition from the Romantic and somewhat rhapsodic mode of his early poems to the more restrained and economical approach of the 'Impressionistic' or Aesthetic style characteristic of his more mature verse. If the Italianate titles of many of Wilde's devotional or Rossettian poems suggested their 'Pre-Raphaelite' influences, the French title betrays the major influence on this and other poems within this genre, an influence which is more painterly than poetic. The painting style known as Impressionism, exemplified by the French painters Monet and Pissaro, was represented in London by the American painter James Abbott McNeill Whistler (1834–1903), sometime friend and sparring-partner of Wilde. Whistler rejected the 'anecdotal' approach to painting, the sacred Victorian tenet that 'every picture tells a story', and advocated instead a more abstract art which rendered the 'impression' of a scene, the combined effects of light, atmospheric conditions and formal relationships. That Wilde (who championed Whistler's work on many occasions) was responding in poetry to Whistler's challenge in painting is suggested by the imagery of his 'Impression du Matin'. The terms 'nocturne' and 'Harmony' (borrowed by Whistler from music, and reflecting his ideal for abstraction) evoke Whistler's painterly idiom. Noctures reproduced the effects of approaching night, generally depicting the river Thames (*Nocturne in Blue and Silver*, 1871, *Nocturne in Blue and Gold – Old Battersea Bridge*, 1872–7), while his Harmonies were often portraits or interior arrangements dominated by certain colours. Wilde's poetic 'Impression' approaches this painterly ideal. Mythological or literary anecdote, drama and allegorical detail (the properties of many of his earlier poems) are mostly avoided. Wilde's earlier poems had featured many dawn scenes, but this is perhaps the first to avoid an allegorical personification of the morning. Instead, like the Impressionistic painter, Wilde is primarily interested in light colour and atmospheric effect. The inclusion of the prostitute in the final stanza does not threaten this, as the allusion is lightly handled and denoted by a few sketched-in details. Significantly, in a later version of this poem which Wilde presented to a friend Luther Munday in 1891, he omitted the third stanza, thus excising the more 'dynamic' features, which threaten the ideal of purely impressionistic description (see Mason, p. 175).

p. 45 Impression: Le Reveillon: first published in *The Irish Monthly*, vol. 5, February 1877 as part 2 of 'Lotus Leaves', it was revised for the 1881 volume. The title refers to both a celebration at Christmas or New Year, and a term used principally in painting to denote a highlighting effect.

p. 45 Impressions: Les Silhouettes ... La Fuite de la Lune: 'Les Silhouettes' was first published in *Pan*, 23 April 1881, and then appeared in the 1881 *Poems*. 'La Fuite de la Lune' (the flight of the moon), was originally part of 'Lotus Leaves' (see note to 'Le reveillon' above); it then appeared with 'Les Silhouettes' in *Pan*, and finally in the 1881 volume. 'Les Silhouettes' is another exercise in the Impressionistic mode, a sketch of colours and light effects, which draws its strength from its economy of detail. In 'La Fuite de la Lune' Wilde has taken material produced when he was still hymning the twin attractions of Classical antiquity and Roman Catholic mysticism, and attempts to fashion its more descriptive passages into an 'impression'. The personification of the moon in the final stanza, however, serves as a reminder of this poem's provenance, notwithstanding the change of title.

p. 46 In the Gold Room: A Harmony: another 'painterly' poem, which first appeared in the 1881 *Poems*. Its subtitle refers to both the subject of the poem, a woman playing a piano, and the arrangement and effect of the poem itself. Each stanza is dominated by a colour – the white of the first moves to gold in the second, and red in the concluding stanza. The poem attempts to 'harmonise' these colours, but also subtly suggests a colour-coded 'thermometer' for the speaker's passions: the colours reflect his increasing attraction for the woman, moving from the chaste detachment of the 'white' stanza, to the fire and blood imagery of the red stanza's physical consummation. This poem reflects Wilde in a transitional stage; it retains a Rossettian element with its 'fleshly' conclusion, and delight in rich colours and their mystical associations, but combines this with a more abstract approach to the arrangement and effect of tones and moods for their own sake. The title evokes similar studies by Whistler, and anticipates the work of the Austrian Symbolist painter Gustav Klimt (1862–1918), whose own palate would be dominated by the colours Wilde employs.

p. 47 Impressions: Le Jardin ... La Mer: 'the garden' and 'the sea'. First published in *Our Continent*, vol. 1, 15 February 1882. In both poems natural phenomena such as petals or waves are compared with more synthetic and artificial objects. This rendering the 'natural' artificial, or challenging the accepted understanding of such terms, would be a characteristic of Wilde's later works such as his 'decadent' novel *The Picture of Dorian Gray* (1890/1), and critical works like 'The Decay of Lying' (1889).

p. 48 Le Jardin des Tuileries: taken from *In a Good Cause* (June, 1885), a charity publication suporting a London children's hospital, hence the subject of the poem. The setting is a Parisian park, close to the Louvre. The idea suggested in the final stanza, that the barren tree should break into Spring blossoms as a consequence of the children playing on it, would be adapted for one of Wilde's most famous fairy stories 'The Selfish Giant' (1888).

p. 49 The Harlot's House: taken from *The Dramatic Review*, vol. 1, 11 April 1885, this poem represents Wilde in his 'Symbolist' phase. Its allegorical association between 'lust' and death, recalls the works of the poet Charles Baudelaire (*Les Fleurs du Mal*, 1857), and the Belgian painter Félicien Rops. The morbid imagery of this poem relies on the association between prostitution and venereal disease. The final image of the dawn as a frightened girl holds great pathos and beauty, and is one of Wilde's more successful and evocative uses of personification. The motif of the *danse macabre*, and some of the rhymes used in this poem would re-surface in the 'phantasmagoria' section of *The Ballad of Reading Gaol* (1897). **l. 6 Treues Liebes Herz**: 'true heart's love' – a waltz by Johann Strauss (1825–99).

p. 50 On the Sale by Auction of Keats' Love Letters: taken from *Sonnets of this Century*, edited by William Sharp, 1886, it also appeared in *The Dramatic Review*, 23 January 1886. The sonnet refers to an actual sale which Wilde attended in 1885. Keats' love for Fanny Brawne remained largely a secret during his short life. In this poem Wilde sets up an opposition between the mercantile ethos which will put a price on anything (whilst knowing the value of nothing), and the hallowed realm of art; a theme he would pursue in many of his critical pronouncements. Wilde further develops the theme of the poet as martyr, and the identification between the

suffering Christ and the poet who suffers ostracism or even martyrdom.
l. 1 Endymion: a poem by Keats, used here to represent the poet as lover.

p. 51 Fantasies Décoratives: Le Panneau ... Les Ballons: taken from
Lady's Pictorial, Christmas 1887, these poems were originally part of
pictorial designs. As their general title suggests, these poems concentrate on
decorative devices. A 'panneau' is a poster or panel, and suggests that what
is being described, despite an element of narrative or 'drama', is a work of
art, and one conspicuous for its artificiality. In this poem, fingernails are like
jewels, ears are like shells, the sun, or at least its reflection, is like a dragon,
and birds appear to be made of metal. The inverted repetition in the final
stanza of the lines from the first, further reinforces the static and 'decorative'
quality of the composition. Similarly, in 'Les Ballons', butterflies appear to
be made of silk and moons of satin, whilst the balloons themselves are
compared with jewels and such natural phenomena as rose leaves and
gossamer. Both poems are ornate exercises in artifice, putting into practice
the aesthetic that Wilde advocated in his criticism.

p. 53 Canzonet: taken from *Art and Letters: An Illustrated review*, vol. 2,
April 1888, the title is a musical term denoting a song or madrigal, but also
an operatic 'aria'. **l. 16 Ambergris**: a secretion used in perfumery.
l. 21 faun: a woodland deity, often associated with, or accompanying the
god Pan.

p. 54 Symphony in Yellow: taken from a publication entitled *The Golden
Grain Guide to the Al Fresco Fayre and Floral Fete*, a charity project to which
Wilde contributed this poem in 1889. The poem is an Impressionistic
cityscape, once more reminiscent of many of Whistler's London scenes –
'symphonies' were also part of the Whistlerian lexicon. (See the introduction to the present volume.) Wilde would produce other studies in yellow,
including an unfinished poem entitled 'La Dame Jaune' (the yellow lady).

p. 54 In The Forest: taken from the *Lady's Pictorial*, Christmas 1889.
Fauns, like Sphinxes were very much a *fin-de-siècle* motif, occurring in
innumerable works of art from the period, from Stéphane Mallarmé's poem
'*Après-midi d'un faune*' (1876), to the grotesque figures found in many of
Aubrey Beardsley's drawings. The imagery of 'In the Forest', with its
allusions to music and madness, evokes the attributes of the woodland
deities, known both for their musical proficiency and their tendency to
riotous hedonism.

p. 55 La Circassienne: 'the Caucasian lady'. The text for this poem is taken from a copy of an unpublished manuscript made in 1907 (see 'Note on the Text'). It is a longer version of a poem entitled 'Remorse (A Study in Saffron)', which Wilde produced for a friend in 1889. 'Remorse' consists of stanzas one, two and five of the present poem (see Collins *Collected Works*, 1994, p. 873). To my knowledge, this is the first time that 'La Circassienne' has appeared in print. Wilde would both extend and shorten poems in the process of revision and in the fullness of time. Therefore whether 'Remorse' is a revised version of 'La Circassienne', or vice versa is difficult to determine. The blue, vermillion and purple details which he introduces in the third and fourth stanzas of the present poem would certainly be inappropriate for a 'study in saffron', and may very well have been excised on this occasion. Or perhaps the sub-title 'study' suggests that 'Remorse' is a mere sketch which was fleshed out in 'La Circassienne'. The postscript 'Cairo' is intriguing, and further complicates the question of dating the poem. As far as it is known, Wilde never visited Egypt. The closest he came to it was when he visited Algiers with Lord Alfred Douglas in 1895 (although a few days are missing from his biography at this point, and at other periods). Douglas himself had been in Cairo in 1894, but it is unlikely that Wilde visited him. The poem itself shows Wilde in the Baudlearian mode; its almost fetishistic focus on the beloved's hair, the jewel imagery, and the celebration of her frosty disdain, recalls such poems as 'Les Bijoux' and 'Le Chevelure'.

p. 56 *The Sphinx*: probably started while Wilde was still a student in Oxford, it was not completed, however, until 1894. The poem was published with Charles Ricketts's illustrations, by John Lane at The Bodley Head – text and image combine in a masterpiece of *fin-de-siècle* book production. The poem is an extended reverie on an *objet d'art* and its mythological associations, and displays Wilde, the word-master, at his most playful and extravagant. The poem manages to combine bizarre (pseudo-) erudition with camp and grotesque humour. The 'student' stretches the resources of his own imagination to its limits, eventually turning from fascination and voyeuristic attraction to repulsion, or perhaps mental exhaustion. The influences on this poem, both literary and pictorial, are numerous. The Sphinx was very much a late nineteenth-century literary and artistic motif. It featured in the ornate prose of Flaubert's *La Tentation de Saint Antoine* (1874), and the paintings of, amongst others, Gustave Moreau ('Oedipus and the Sphinx', 1864) and Franz Von Struck ('The Sphinx', 1895). Wilde had earlier used the image in his short story 'The Sphinx without a Secret: An Etching' (1891). *The Sphinx* combines the erudition and dark sexuality of Flaubert's novel with the bejewelled exotica of Moreau's painting. The idiom of the poem is allusive, erudite and esoteric almost to the point of absurdity. Therefore to annotate it and provide a gloss for every obscure reference would be both pedantic and self-defeating. So many of the words were chosen almost exclusively for their sound or 'colour'. The sense of the word was often a secondary consideration, if a consideration at all. This also goes for the accuracy of his scholarship. Exact definitions for words would detract from rather than enhance the effect of this poem, which is to swathe its object in an aura of mythical and mystical association. Many words will, therefore, be allowed to remain in obscurity, retaining a vagueness appropriate to Wilde's 'decadent' reverie. References which, in the present editor's opinion, enhance the meaning of the poem, or which could otherwise cause confusion, are glossed. **Sphinx**: a mythological beast, who, in the Greek tradition, had the head and breasts of a woman, the body of a lion, the wings of a bird, and the tail of a serpent. She inhabited Thebes, and is associated with the legend of Oedipus, the one man who could solve her riddle, and escape being devoured by her. **l. 22 the Egyptian**: Cleopatra, queen of Egypt (68–30 b.c.), who formed an alliance with Mark Antony, Julius Caesar's consul (these lovers were the subject of Shakespeare's history *Antony and Cleopatra*). **l. 25 Cyprian**: Venus, lover of Adonis. **l. 25 catafalque**: a structure to support a coffin for a funeral ceremony. **l. 31 Jewish maid**: refers to Mary mother of Jesus, and is based loosely on the story of the flight to Egypt from the persecution of Herod, as told in Matthew, 2:14. **l. 37 labyrinth ... twy-formed Bull**: the famous maze built at Crete by Daedalus to house the Minotaur, who was half bull and half human. **l. 40 mandragores**: plants with narcotic, but also aphrodisiac properties, suitable embellishments for a poem steeped in an atmosphere of reverie and heady eroticism. **l. 46 leman**: lover. **l. 51 Chimaera**: like the Sphinx, a composite monster. **l. 62 Lúpanar**: brothel. **l. 67 the Tyrian**: Adonis. **l. 69 hawk-faced head**: Ra, an Assyrian deity. **l. 74 Ammon**: is the principal paramour for the Sphinx in the student's imagination. He was the Libyan equivalent of the Greek god Zeus. **l. 83 oracles**: god's prophecies, usually in answer to specific requests. The most famous oracle in Antiquity belonged to Apollo at Delphi. **l. 98 Colchian witch**: Medea, in Greek legend, was a witch who aided Jason in his quest for the Golden Fleece. **l. 120 Titan thews**: giant limbs. **l. 120 paladin**: a courtier or officer of a palace. **l. 126 spikenard**: an aromatic plant or the perfume derived from it. **l. 135 Nilus**: a personification of the River Nile. **l. 159 grey, gilt-dialled towers**: of the college where the student contemplates the Sphinx. This description certainly fits Wilde's own college Magdalen, the chapel tower of which is still tipped with golden vanes. **l. 162 poppy-drowsy Queen**: Persephone or Proserpine. **l. 170 Atys**: in Greek mythology a youth who in a fit of madness castrated himself (but with a stone, not a knife).

p. 66 The Ballad of Reading Gaol: Wilde's final poem; it was also his last work of art. In May 1895 Wilde was sentenced to two years imprisonment with hard labour for what were known as 'acts of gross indecency with other male persons'. He served most of his term at Reading Gaol. On release in May 1897 Wilde went immediately to France, changing his name to Sebastian Melmoth (a composite of the martyr St Sebastian, and the Gothic figure Melmoth created by his great uncle Charles Robert Maturin in his novel *Melmoth the Wanderer*, 1820). Wilde never returned to England, wandering the Continent until his death in November 1900. Wilde started work on *The Ballad* shortly after his release. It was published anonymously in February 1898. **C.3.3** was Wilde's cell number at Reading. Wilde's name appeared for the first time in brackets in the seventh edition (1899). The text is taken from the second edition, the last to be revised by the author. The poem tells of the horrors of prison life, and offers a challenge to those who are authorised to punish their fellow humans (see also Wilde's letters to *The Daily Chronicle* on this subject, reproduced in *Letters*, pp. 568–74 and 722–26). Whilst the poem is in many ways a departure from Wilde's earlier poetic style, as conspicuous for its didactic 'sincerity' as his earlier poems were for their amoral artificiality, it is nonetheless still recognisably Wildean. An emphasis on suffering was always a feature of his art. From the poet as martyr in 'Sonnet to Liberty', 'The Grave of Keats' and 'On the Sale by Auction of Keats' Love Letters', to so many of the fairy stories such as the 'Nightingale and the Rose', Wilde found beauty as well as pathos in portraying and identifying with the suffering of others. The phantasmagoria endured by the prisoners on the condemned man's last night recalls the *danse macabre* of 'The Harlot's House'. On the whole, however, the poem is more direct than his earlier works, while the allusions tend to be Biblical rather than classical, reflecting its moral purpose. **In Memoriam C. T. W.**: the poem is dedicated to Charles Thomas Wooldridge, who was sentenced to death for slitting his wife's throat. Wooldridge's death by hanging at Reading Gaol provides the 'occasion' for Wilde's *Ballad*. **l. 41 The coward does it with a kiss**: the kiss of Judas Iscariot, one of Christ's disciples, who betrayed him with a kiss (see *Matthew*, 26:49). **l. 96 Caiaphas**: the high-priest in Jerusalem who bribed Judas to hand Jesus over to the authorities. **l. 118 anodyne**: a curative. **l. 173 iron gin**: a trap. **l. 211 around the ring**: the prisoners' exercise yard, one of which was famously depicted in Vincent Van Gogh's painting *La Ronde des Prisonniers*. **l. 217 tarry rope**: 'hard labour' in prison usually involved oakum picking, the unravelling of old ropes which were used to stop up the seams of wooden boats to prevent leaks. Other tasks performed by the prisoners are referred to in the following stanza. **l. 278 Mad mourners of a corse**: a corpse. **l. 291 riga-doon**: a dance popular in the eighteenth century. **l. 321 demirep**: a woman of dubious reputation. **l. 434 crooked arrows starred**: the official dress issued to prisoners was marked with inverted arrows. **ll. 485–6 the barren staff . . . the great Pope's sight**: in the legend of Tannhäuser, the knight spends a year with Venus in her hill. When he attempts absolution from Pope Urban IV, the Pope refuses it, claiming that he is as likely to be forgiven his sins as his dry staff blossoming once more. The staff blossoms, but the knight has returned to the Venusburg. The theme was popular with poets and artists in the late nineteenth century, including Swinburne, Aubrey Beardsley, Wagner and Burne-Jones. It is used here as an example of forgiveness, and supports the central theme of the poem that God forgives where man condemns. **l. 543 Since first Man took his brother's life**: Cain in the Book of Genesis was the first murderer, killing his brother Abel.

Glossary of Classical Allusions

ACTÆON, a hunter who accidentally spied on the goddess Artemis while she bathed. As a punishment he was transformed into a stag, and torn apart by his own hounds.

ADONIS, a beautiful youth who, in one tradition, is wooed by Aphrodite.

APHRODITE, the Greek goddess of love, called Venus in Roman myths.

ARCADY or ARCADIA, a region of Greece, the importance of which is more symbolic and poetical than geographical or historical. In poetry, the region has come to denote an ideal realm of pastoral simplicity, and has associations with the 'Golden Age'.

ARTEMIS, Greek goddess of the hunt, and traditionally depicted as a virgin.

ATHENA, Greek goddess who was also patron of Athens, the city which bore her name.

DIANA, the Roman equivalent of Artemis.

DIONYSUS, Greek god of wine and ecstasy. His worship is associated with revelry, riot and even madness.

EROS, the god of love, called Cupid by the Romans.

ENDYMION, a beautiful youth who was loved by the moon. He was put into a perpetual sleep, and every night the moon (Cynthia or Diana) embraced him. The title of a poem by John Keats who treated this theme.

HERACLES, called Hercules in Roman mythology, he was famous for his strength and his feats of bravery.

HYACINTH, a beautiful youth beloved of Apollo, accidentally killed by the god when his discus struck him.

NARCISSUS, a beautiful youth who spurned all suitors, and fell in love with his own reflection in a pool.

PAN, in Greek mythology he is the god of flocks and shepherds, and associated with Arcadia. He is renowned for his musical ability.

PERSEPHONE or PROSERPINE, Persephone is the name given by the Greeks to the queen of the Underworld (Proserpine is the Roman name). A goddess who was daughter of Zeus and Demeter (the corn goddess), she was carried off by Hades and forced to spend six months of each year with him in the Underworld.

SATYRS, *woodland demi-gods, who were half men and half goats. Renowned for their lewdness and drunken revelry. Often attendants to Dionysus.*

Select Bibliography and Suggestions for Further Reading

Karl Beckson, *Oscar Wilde: The Critical Heritage* (London: Routledge, 1970).

Harold Bloom, ed., *Oscar Wilde* (New York: Chelsea House, 1985).

Eckardt, Gilman and Chamberlin, *Oscar Wilde's London* (London: Michael O'Mara, 1988).

Richard Ellmann, *Oscar Wilde* (London: Hamish Hamilton, 1987).

Reginia Gagnier, ed., *Oscar Wilde: Critical Essays* (New York: G. K. Hall, 1991).

William Gaunt, *The Aesthetic Adventure* (London: Cardinal, 1988).

Rupert Hart-Davis, ed., *The Letters of Oscar Wilde* (London: Rupert Hart-Davis, 1962).

Rupert Hart-Davis, ed., *More Letters of Oscar Wilde* (London: John Murray, 1985).

Stuart Mason (Christopher Millard), *Bibliography of Oscar Wilde* (London: T. Werner Laurie, 1914).

E. H. Mikhail, *Oscar Wilde: An Annotated Bibliography of Criticism* (London: Macmillan, 1978).

Walter Pater, 'Poems by William Morris', *Westminster Review*, 90 (October 1868), pp. 300–312.

Peter Raby, *Oscar Wilde* (Cambridge: Cambridge University Press, 1988).

Oscar Wilde, *Intentions* (London: Osgood, McIlvaine & Co., 1891).

Oscar Wilde, *Complete Works of Oscar Wilde* (Glasgow: Harper Collins, 1994).

Acknowledgements

I would like to thank the following institutions for their help in preparing this edition, and for allowing me to make use of manuscripts. The Master and Fellows of University College, Oxford; The William Andrews Clark Memorial Library; University of California, Los Angeles; The British Library; The Bodleian Library, Oxford. I would especially like to acknowledge my gratitude to the Estate of Oscar Wilde, represented with great warmth and scholarly acumen by his grandson Merlin Holland.

Everyman's Poetry

Titles available in this series all at £1.00

William Blake
ed. Peter Butter
0 460 87800 X

Robert Burns
ed. Donald Low
0 460 87814 X

Samuel Taylor Coleridge
ed. John Beer
0 460 87826 3

Thomas Gray
ed. Robert Mack
0 460 87805 0

Ivor Gurney
ed. George Walter
0 460 87797 6

George Herbert
ed. D. J. Enright
0 460 87795 X

Robert Herrick
ed. Douglas Brooks-Davies
0 460 87799 2

John Keats
ed. Nicholas Roe
0 460 87808 5

**Henry Wadsworth
Longfellow**
ed. Anthony Thwaite
0 460 87821 2

John Milton
ed. Gordon Campbell
0 460 87813 1

Edgar Allan Poe
ed. Richard Gray
0 460 87804 2

Poetry Please!
Foreword by Charles
Causley
0 460 87824 7

Alexander Pope
ed. Douglas Brooks-Davies
0 460 87798 4

Lord Rochester
ed. Paddy Lyons
0 460 87819 0

Christina Rossetti
ed. Jan Marsh
0 460 87820 4

William Shakespeare
ed. Martin Dodsworth
0 460 87815 8

Alfred, Lord Tennyson
ed. Michael Baron
0 460 87802 6

R. S. Thomas
ed. Anthony Thwaite
0 460 87811 5

Walt Whitman
ed. Ellman Crasnow
0 460 87825 5

Oscar Wilde
ed. Robert Mighall
0 460 87803 4